Prayer 101

This book is dedicated
to the members of Liberty Baptist Church
in Palatka, Florida.
This group of saints really knows how to pray.

Prayer 101

Learning
to
Talk
with
God

DON M. AYCOCK

CHALICE
PRESS
ST. LOUIS, MISSOURI

Cover art: Getty Images
Cover and interior design: Elizabeth Wright

Visit Chalice Press on the World Wide Web at
www.chalicepress.com

10 9 8 7 6 5 4 3 2 1   06 07 08 09 10 11

Library of Congress Cataloging-in-Publication Data

Aycock, Don M.
    Prayer 101 : learning to talk with God / Don M. Aycock.
        p. cm.
    Includes bibliographical references.
    ISBN-13: 978-0-8272-2987-7 (pbk. : alk. paper)
    ISBN-10: 0-8272-2987-9 (pbk. : alk. paper)
    1. Prayer—Christianity. I. Title: Prayer one hundred one. II. Title:
Prayer one hundred and one. III. Title.
    BV215.A97 2006
    248.3'2—dc22
                                                    2006006281

Printed in the United States of America

Contents

Foreword

Prayer 101 has the capacity to help us become more effective in talking with God—and from the looks of things, we can really use the help.

After living with Jesus Christ and seeing how he prayed, the disciples said, "Lord, teach us to pray." They realized their poor, stumbling efforts resembled in no way the powerful communication Jesus had with his Heavenly Father.

Don Aycock tells us that 75 percent of Americans say they believe in prayer. But the highest divorce rate in the world, illegal drug usage at every level of society, and a rising level of anger reveal a different picture. Something is terribly wrong.

While watching a drama on television, I saw the following take place:

A woman sits across from a friend in a small café. She asks, "Is there any hope for you?"

The man she's talking to shakes his head and starts to cry. "No, I've tried everything possible. I guess all I can do now is pray."

The woman places her hand on his shoulder and says, with obvious sympathy, "Oh! You poor soul!"

Is that all we think of prayer? Is it only a hopeless plea to be tossed out toward an unfamiliar God when nothing else can be done? Are our expectations really that low?

I drive a car to work every day, but that doesn't mean I understand how it works. I can change a tire, add fluids, and wash my vehicle. If it breaks down, however, I'm not one of those individuals who open the hood and save tons of money by repairing it themselves. I'm at the mercy of the local garage.

In the same way, prayer seems to be a mystery to many people. They may use it every day, or they may only heave up a desperate call to heaven when they're backed into a corner. In any case, they have a poor understanding of this wonderful privilege God gives us to bring our needs before him.

So, do we really need to learn how to pray?

Christ's response would be a resounding, "Yes!" He gave his disciples a model for prayer. (We call this the "Lord's Prayer.") The longest book in the Bible is Psalms, ancient songs that are, in many cases, prayers set to music. From these examples, God wants us to learn how to pray properly and effectively.

What about the author of this book on prayer? Can he really help us learn more about this important aspect of the Christian life?

The true test of a Christian is how straight he or she walks with God in every situation. I have known Don Aycock for more than twenty years. A gifted writer and speaker, a flawless guitarist and a loving pastor, Don has stood firm in his faith during good times, physical ailments, and spiritually trying moments. In short, Don has lived out what he writes about in this book. He's a man who practices what he preaches.

One other note: The second chapter, "A Stubborn Misunderstanding of Prayer," is worth the price of the entire book.

When you turn this page, you could be taking the first step in having your life changed. Apply the truths you read in *Prayer 101* and your relationship with Jesus Christ has the potential of becoming richer and more fulfilling, as you understand better how to communicate with God almighty.

MARK SUTTON
Pastor, Brookwood Baptist Church
Shreveport, Louisiana

Introduction

The ancient Roman word *precarious* originally meant, "obtained by prayer or begging." Today something that is dependent on anything uncertain is called "precarious." That is what some people think prayer is—a last resort; a beggar's choice; a weakling's fallback. For all of the misunderstandings and even deliberate attacks on prayer, one fact is certain—people pray. A Gallup poll revealed that over 75 percent of Americans pray.[1] That is an astounding number considering that less than 25 percent of Americans regularly go to worship services. Regardless of their outward religiosity, people still reach out to God in prayer. They want some contact with Truth and to know that life makes some sort of sense.

Blaise Pascal, a seventeenth-century mathematician and philosopher, was right. He wrote, "The heart has its reasons, of which reason knows nothing; we know this in countless ways."[2] We may not be able to give an adequate explanation for our urges to pray, but our "heart has its reasons." We *feel* it is the right thing to do. That feeling, that urge to reach out beyond ourselves is God-given. We might call it a "homing" instinct. It is what helps you want to read this book and do something about it.

I will not be spending much time in this book defending prayer. Other books do that. I will be walking with you, much like a guide on a tour, as we move through this country called "prayer." Like a group of tourists, we will concentrate on seeing the highlights and will not linger very long in any one place. We will look at what prayer is *not*. By learning what it is not, we will be in a better position to learn what it is. Then we will examine several key passages of scripture and open them up to discover what prayer does to us and to those around us. Please read all the scripture passages that are printed throughout this book. They will prepare you to understand the discussion in each chapter better.

The "bottom line" for many people regarding prayer is this. They want to know, "Can prayer actually *do* something to make my life different and better?" We explore this question in different ways in the pages that follow. Right now, though, I want to give you a personal illustration of what prayer can do for us.

In July of 2000 I had an accident that forced me to raise the issue. I have very little memory of the event itself, though I recall the steps up to that moment. We had moved into a house with a large play set in the yard. It contained a wooden structure with a slide, ladders, and swings. Our children were grown, so we offered it to our church's youth pastor. One day he brought a group of adults and youth to dismantle it and take it to his house. One on the adults, Lance, brought a chain saw in case he needed it to cut the posts off at the ground. He noticed that a large limb had been broken on an oak tree in the yard. It was still attached to the tree, although most of it was on the ground. I had been away at a conference and had left the limb for later and had felt no hurry to remove it. The man got his saw and began cutting.

Carla, my wife, and I had gone out for lunch before the group got there. When we arrived back home, I got my saw and went out to help cut the limb. I have had a chain saw for years and have great respect (read this as fear) of them. They can hurt you if you are not very careful. I had looked at the limb earlier and realized it had twisted a bit when it fell. I knew it had some torque on it so we wanted to be careful.

We began cutting at the end of the limb, piling the brush out of the way as we went. As we got about half way to the trunk of the tree, Lance got his saw pinched in the limb. A chainsaw has a tendency to get stuck in wood if that wood moves slightly. He was in front of me so I handed him my saw and took hold of his so he could cut around it and free it.

I have no memory of what happened next, but Lance explained it this way. When he began cutting the limb to free his saw, the limb broke off the tree and fell the rest of the way. It was about twelve inches in diameter so it fell with great force. As it was falling it whipped around hitting me in the legs and knocking me flat. It hit the ground, bounced up over Lance and came back down on my head while I was still on my back.

Bang. Just like that I had a fractured skull and a brain injury.

I can remember hearing the blow but not feeling it. I remember the sensation of facing the sun although my eyes were closed. I felt nothing at that point. That was soon to change. When I came back to consciousness, everyone was kneeling around me placing ice on my head. Lance told me later that he feared that the limb had killed me because of how it hit me and because I was so still. The ambulance arrived and the medics tried to put me onto a board to transfer me to the ambulance. I began to feel some discomfort in my neck but it was nothing too great. I have always had a high tolerance for pain so I did not worry about it. When the medics tried to move me, a searing pain shot through my neck as if someone had stabbed me with an ice pick. I could not move my right arm much so I told the men to wait a moment. I reached behind me and held my neck with my left hand to give me some stability. They finally got me moved to the stretcher but I discovered that any movement hurt me worse than anything I have ever experienced.

The ambulance took me to our local hospital. It has a great staff and the Emergency Room is well equipped for its size. The E.R. doctor examined me and informed me that because I had lost consciousness they were going to send me to a trauma hospital in Jacksonville, about fifty miles away. He said, "The helicopter is already on the way."

The "chopper" arrived and the attendants shuttled me to it for the fifteen-minute flight to Jacksonville. They started an IV and took vital signs. About halfway into the flight I told the medic that I was going to throw up. He grabbed a bucket and I baptized him and his chopper.

Meanwhile, our youth pastor, Neal, knew how to get to the hospital by back roads. He drove Carla to Jacksonville and arrived almost as soon as I did. The trauma team examined me and sent me to get an MRI. I had begun to fade a bit. The last thing I remember was being loaded into that machine and telling the attendant that I was going to throw up. She said the dumbest thing I've ever heard in the hospital: "Don't do that. Just lie still." I did not obey so I baptized her and her million-dollar machine. That was the last thing I knew until the next day.

The MRI showed that I had a fractured skull and blood clots forming on the brain. I woke up in the Intensive Care Unit. Everything was fuzzy for a while but I realized I had a huge bandage on my head. The neurosurgeon had operated and removed an area of my skull about the size of my fist. This gave him the room to remove the blood clots and stop the bleeding. He attached the skull back together with small titanium clips and screws and then stapled my scalp closed. I made good progress for two days. The doctor even talked about letting me go home soon. On the third day trouble developed.

When I woke up on the third morning I notice a slight pressure in my head. I opened my mouth to talk to the nurse and nothing but gibberish came out. I could not speak. Carla arrived soon, listened to me for a minute, and then went out to find the nurse. She said, "Something is wrong." The nurse explained that she had already called the neurosurgeon and he was on his way. When he got there he sent me for tests and found that I was bleeding from the brain again. We went back to surgery and repeated the earlier process.

Several more days in ICU were needed to get me to the point I could be moved to a regular room. Most of that time is hazy, although I remember bits of it. I realized that most of my trouble was not with my head but with my neck and right arm. No one seemed to pay any attention to my complaints about terrible pain or my inability to use my right arm. Any time anyone tried to move me, I had to reach up and support my neck. Even then the pain would shoot through me as if someone held a branding iron to my back.

I could not talk and I could not write. What a predicament for a preacher and writer to be in! Only after undergoing speech and physical therapy did I regain full speech and use of my right arm. I am so grateful to be able to live a normal life again. But there were days when I wondered what lay in store for me. Would I walk again? Could I write? Would I able to speak again?

In the midst of all this, everyone I knew was praying for my recovery. All my family, friends scattered around the country, and especially my church all asked God to spare my life and more than that—to make me well again. Many people said to me, "Don, I've never prayed so much in all my life!" Today, I am well and have virtually no after-affects from the accident, aside from a whopper of a scar on my head. Never before or since have I been the recipient of such concentrated prayer. Did prayer heal me? No, prayer did not heal me in the sense of some automatic response. God healed me, but I do believe that God heard the petitions of everyone on my behalf. That is why I can write these words you are reading now. What prayer did was to give the divine "Yes" to my life. (See 2 Cor. 1:19.)

I do not write as an "expert" on prayer. I am a struggling pilgrim just as you are. My journey has included serving as a pastor for many years, being a writer for longer than that, and working as an employee for a national denominational ministry. This last assignment allowed me to travel across the country and get to know many people. I discovered that people everywhere are struggling and working in an effort to know what God wants and to carry it out. Author Anne-Sophie Swetchine has written, "Providence has hidden a charm in difficult undertakings, which is appreciated only by those who dare to grapple with them."[3]

Yes, prayer matters. It *does* something. Now let us examine just what it does and "dare to grapple" with our findings.

1

You Are Invited to Pray

*One day Jesus was praying in a certain place. When he
finished, one of his disciples said to him, "Lord, teach us
to pray, just as John taught his disciples."*
   He said to them, "When you pray, say:
     'Father,
     hallowed be your name,
     your kingdom come.
    Give us each day our daily bread.
    Forgive us our sins,
     for we also forgive everyone who sins against us.
    And lead us not into temptation.'"

*Then he said to them, "Suppose one of you has a
friend, and he goes to him at midnight and says, 'Friend,
lend me three loaves of bread, because a friend of mine on
a journey has come to me, and I have nothing to set
before him.'*
   *"Then the one inside answers, 'Don't bother me. The
door is already locked, and my children are with me in
bed. I can't get up and give you anything.' I tell you,
though he will not get up and give him the bread because
he is his friend, yet because of the man's boldness he will
get up and give him as much as he needs.*

"So I say to you: Ask and it will be given to you; seek and you will find; knock and the door will be opened to you. For everyone who asks receives; he who seeks finds; and to him who knocks, the door will be opened.

"Which of you fathers, if your son asks for a fish, will give him a snake instead? Or if he asks for an egg, will give him a scorpion? If you then, though you are evil, know how to give good gifts to your children, how much more will your Father in heaven give the Holy Spirit to those who ask him!"

LUKE 11:1–13

Dear Friend, You are cordially invited to attend a meeting between you and God. The time is flexible, and you may accept this invitation as early as five minutes from now. Your Host is awaiting your reply. Please do not be long.

If this invitation arrived in your mailbox, how would you respond? My first response would be to check the postmark! Aside from that, we might wonder who would send such an invitation. Imagine it—an invitation from God.

God has actually given us an invitation like that. The whole concept of prayer is based on this one fact: *God wants to communicate with us.* That overriding fact needs to be kept in mind as we think about prayer. To pray is to risk. The acclaimed author of *Roots,* Alex Haley, once said about taking risks:

Nothing is more important. Too often we are taught how *not* to take risks. When we are children in school, for example, we are told to respect our heroes, our founders, and the great people of the past. We are directed to their portraits hanging on walls and in hallways and reproduced in textbooks. What we are not told is that these leaders, who look so serene and secure in those portraits, were rule-*breakers.* They were risk-takers in the best sense of the word; they dared to be different.[1]

Be a risk-taker. Learn to pray.

A Normal Request

"[O]ne of his disciples said to him, 'Lord, teach us to pray.'" From that simple request came Jesus' teaching on prayer. The disciple, who is unnamed here, had noticed that prayer characterized Jesus' life. He wanted the Lord to pass on to him and the other disciples his teachings about prayer. Religious guides and rabbis of that day taught their followers how to pray. The disciple knew this because his request included the words, "as John taught his disciples."

This is the beginning point of genuine prayer—a desire to reach out to God. The real quest of prayer is to know God, and not to get stuff. How different this is from the "name-it-and-claim-it" mentality that sees religious faith as a fast lane to riches! Recently I received a bulk mail letter addressed to "Someone Connected with This Address." That made me suspicious from the beginning. Inside was a letter telling me that God was going to bless me if I did what the letter said. Enclosed was a sheet of folded paper that was called a "prayer rug." I was supposed to kneel on this "rug" and check off my needs on the back of the letter. Those needs included everything from "my soul" to asking "God to bless me with this amount of money," complete with a blank space for me to fill in the amount. Then—and here is the clincher—I was to mail back the "prayer rug" and the letter with my prayer needs checked along with a "seed gift" (read that as a financial contribution) for this organization.

I have never heard of the group that sent this letter and I do not know if they are really legitimate or not. The letter and the "prayer rug" strike me as a scam. At the very least, it seems to turn prayer into a commodity that can be purchased. Is that what Jesus intended when he taught the disciples to pray?

Prayer is intimate interpersonal communication between a person and God. This communication builds a personal relationship with God. David Whyte uses an illustration from marriage to shed some light on this topic. He says that in a normal marriage the man is often frustrated with his wife by her need to talk again about the same thing they talked about recently. That topic of conversation often involves their relationship. The man wonders why they can't just have one big conversation about the relationship and then let it rest for a year or so. Whyte says, "This ongoing, robust conversation he has been having with his wife is not about the relationship. The conversation *is* the relationship."[2]

Susan Scott, in her magnificent book *Fierce Conversations* reflects on David Whyte's comments.

> *The conversation is the relationship.* If the conversation stops, all of the possibilities for the relationship become smaller and all of the possibilities for the individuals in the relationship become smaller, until one day we overhear ourselves in midsentence, making *ourselves* smaller in every encounter, behaving as if we are just the space around our shoes, engaged in yet another three-minute conversation so empty of meaning it crackles.[3]

What a great insight! What is true of human relationships is true of the God-human relationship. To develop the relationship and to keep it growing we need to have what Susan Scott calls "fierce conversations" with God. Do not let this term throw you off. We might think of "fierce" as suggesting menacing, cruel, barbarous, or threatening. But Scott goes to *Roget's Thesaurus* to find words that define her meaning: "the word *fierce* has the following synonyms: robust, intense, strong, powerful, passionate, eager, unbridled, uncurbed, untamed. In the simplest form, *a fierce conversation is one in which we come out from behind ourselves into the conversation and make it real.*"[4]

Think of prayer as a fierce conversation with God. All of the open intimacy implied in communication is present. This includes everything from humor to anger, from request to praise. In prayer we can talk to God as we address another person. When I was a child, for example, I used to tell God jokes. (Then someone spoiled this for me and pointed out that God already knew the punch line.)

Jesus demonstrated the ongoing habit of prayer in his life. His disciples watched him closely and observed the rhythms of His life. At times Jesus was with the public teaching and healing. At other times, he withdrew into solitude with his Father. Apparently the disciples wanted Jesus to teach them a series of words they could use or a pattern of the sort of prayer that God hears. They realized there is a difference between *saying prayers*, which they did, and *actively praying*, which they did not do. The former is saying words. The latter is communicating with the Heavenly Father in dialogue.

The observance of Jesus' habit of prayer caused the disciples to ask for guidance in their prayer lives. A good habit that is observed by others can be helpful to them. A person who is seen going to church each week, for example, might be helpful to motivate others to attend also. If someone is known as a praying person, others might call on that person for help and guidance. We do not want to flaunt our religious life, however. Jesus told a parable about a Pharisee and a tax gatherer to demonstrate this fact. (See Lk. 18:9–14.) We may, however, ask God to teach us to pray.

Let us realize that many ways and forms of prayer exist. There is no one correct way to pray. One scholar looked through the Bible and discovered a wide variety of prayer forms and modes. He wrote:

> Now this general principle has its special application to prayer. Nothing could be more intensely individual than the prayers of the Bible. Nobody tries to commune with God in someone else's way. Some pray kneeling, like Paul (Acts 20:36); some standing, like Jeremiah (Jer. 18:20); some sitting, like David (2 Sam. 7:18); some prostrate, like Jesus (Mt. 26:39). Some pray silently, like Hannah (1 Sam. 1:13); some aloud, like Ezekiel (Ezek. 11:13). Some pray in the temple (2 Kings 19:14); some in bed (Ps. 63:6); in the fields (Gen. 24:11, 12); the hillside (Gen. 28:18–20); on the battlefield (1 Sam. 7:5); by a riverside (Acts 16:13); on the seashore (Acts 21:5); the privacy of the chamber (Mt. 6:6). Moreover all sorts temperaments are found at prayer; practical leaders like Nehemiah, who…seeks God's help before he speaks to the king (Neh. 1:3, 5); poets like the writer of the twenty-seventh Psalm, who love communion with God; men of melancholic mind like Jeremiah, "Hast thou utterly rejected Judah? Hath thy soul loathed Zion?" (Jer. 14:19); and men of radiant spirit like Isaiah, "Jehovah, even Jehovah, is my strength and song; and he is become my

salvation" (Isa. 12:2). There are as many different ways of praying as there are different individuals...We need always to remember, therefore, that there is no mould of prayer into which our communion with God must be run. Let each man pray as best he can."[5]

Why spend our time in such an effort? What is the purpose of prayer? Donald Bloesch, a theologian, has answered this question succinctly:

> The ultimate goal of the life of prayer is the glorification of God and the advancement of his kingdom. Indeed, kingdom service is precisely what gives glory to God. To pray that the glory of God might be made manifest among people in the world is to pray for the fulfillment of God's highest will. It means to pray for the dawning of a new age, when all people may come to know the reality and sovereignty of God (Isa. 66:18; Phil. 2:10, 11; 1 Pet. 4:11).[6]

Our prayers are part of the means of having God's rule spread throughout the world.

Prayer and Persistence

A question is often raised: "Why doesn't God answer our prayers?" Jesus knew this question, too. In teaching his disciples to pray, he addressed the issue of unanswered prayer by telling a parable about a friend who wakes up a neighbor in the middle of the night in order to get provisions for a traveler. Hospitality was considered a sacred duty in that era.

The setting is small village life in Jesus' time. Common people slept in small, one-room houses. The family slept on a raised platform and the domestic animals slept on the bare earthen floor. When a family and livestock were bedded down for the night, no one could get up easily without disturbing everyone. That explains the man's reluctance to get up at midnight: "Don't bother me. The door is already locked, and my children are with me in bed; I can't get up and give you anything" (Lk. 11: 7).

Even so, his friend continues to knock until the man gets up and lends him three loaves. Jesus made his point in verse 8: "I tell you, though he will not get up and give him the bread because he is his friend, yet because of the man's persistence he will get up and give him as much as he needs." The word *persistence* is the key. The word in the original language meant shamelessness. The friend outside has put his duty to his traveling guest above his own need to act "normal." His act was shameless. Even so, he felt that he must do this.

The point Jesus was making had to do with His teaching on prayer. If an ordinary man can be moved by persistence, then Almighty God can be moved by it also. One person has said, "We must not play at prayer, but must show persistence if we do not receive the answer immediately. It is not that God is unwilling and must be pressed into answering," but rather, "if we do not want what we are asking for enough to be persistent, we do not want it very much. It is not such tepid prayer that is answered."[7] People who pray persistently show they have accepted God's invitation to a lifestyle of prayer.

Without persistence we would live as many who Theodore Roosevelt describes as being "in the gray twilight that knows not victory or defeat."[8]

Ask, Seek, Knock

How would you like a money-saving special on prayer? Ridiculous, you say? I actually saw one in a local paper a few years ago. A person calling herself Sister Roberts placed a quarter-page ad in a newspaper. That ad read in part:

> The Southern Born Spiritualist who brings you the solutions to the mysteries of the Deep South, seeks to help many thousands of people who have been Crossed, Have Spells, Can't Hold Money, Want Luck…If you are seeking a sure-fire woman to Aid in Peace, Love and Prosperity in the home, you need to see this woman of God today! [After pointing out how close to God she was, the lady closed with these words in big bold type:] Special This Week: All readings only $5.00 each.[9]

When Jesus said, "Ask, seek, knock," did he mean anything like that? Are we "guaranteed" anything beyond God's care? A look at the original words in this text will help us answer these questions. The words *ask, seek,* and *knock* in the Greek language are present imperatives. A present imperative is a command to continuous asking. Jesus thus said to the disciples, "Keep on asking, keep on seeking, keep on knocking."[10] One quick prayer ripped off in a moment of need may or may not be answered. Jesus' point is that we can be assured of God's answer as we continue to seek God's will. Some answers come only after much effort and patience.

We have many needs because life is so unpredictable. This notice appeared in the window of a coat store in Nottingham, England:

> We have been established for over 100 years and been pleasing and displeasing customers ever since. We have made money and lost money, suffered the effects of coal nationalization, coal rationing, government control, and bad payers. We have been cussed and discussed, messed about, lied to, held up, robbed, and swindled. The only reason we stay in business is to see what happens next.

I can relate to that, can't you? We are wholly right in asking for God's guidance, help, and protection. Some things cannot be planned or avoided in advance. A story is told that comedienne Gracie Allen once received a small, live alligator as a gag. She did not know what else to do with it so she put it in the bathtub and left for an appointment. When Gracie returned, she found this note from her maid: "Dear Miss Allen: Sorry, but I have quit. I don't work in houses where there is an alligator. I'd a told you this when I took on, but I never thought it would come up."[11]

A question might be put to all persons who pray: "What do you want and how badly do you want it?" Verses 9 and 10 suggest that those who want God, and will persist until they know God, will eventually succeed. God invites us to a lifestyle of prayer in which we will continually ask, seek, and knock. This keeps prayer in the realm of personal relationships. This is quite different from thinking of it as a celestial candy machine in which we drop in a prayer, and out pops the prize.

Look carefully at verse 10. Jesus said, "For everyone who asks receives; and he who seeks finds; and to him who knocks, the door will be opened." People who develop a life-long habit of prayer find that they move closer and closer to what God intends for them. They seek, not their own wills, but God's will. They ask, not for merely selfish goals, but for God's goals. They knock in order to receive what is best for themselves in the long run and not the short term. One commentator has noted about verse 10, "God does not have to be waked or cajoled into giving us what we need—many gifts he bestows on the ungodly and ungrateful; but his choicest blessings are reserved for those who will value them and who show their appreciation by asking until they receive."[12]

A story is told about the ancient Greek philosopher Socrates. A young man went to him and said, "Be my teacher. I want to learn everything you know." Socrates took the young man down to the Mediterranean Sea and pushed him under the water and held him a while. When he pulled him up Socrates asked the young man, "What do you want?" The man said, "I want to learn." The teacher pushed him under again, held him longer, and again asked what he wanted. His answer still was, "I want to learn." Finally Socrates held him under for a long while. When he pulled him up and asked, "What do you want?" The young man shouted, "I want air!" The philosopher said, "When you want learning as much as you want air, then you will be ready to study with me."

God desires that we be hungry to learn from him and to know him personally. This takes both time and effort. God invites us to pray, but God will not make us pray. When we are hungry to know God, we will find him.

Getting Good Gifts

"Something good is going to happen to you today!" Does that sound familiar? A televangelist used to say that each time he was on the air. His motto was vaguely biblical. Jesus did promise blessings for his followers, but the followers might not even be aware of the blessings. Even so, God can be trusted to do what is necessary for his people.

Jesus posed an "if-then" situation. If a child asked his father for a fish, what cruel father would give the child a snake instead? If the hungry youngster wanted an egg, would any father hand him a scorpion? The implied answer to these questions is, "No!"

I am the father of twin boys who are pursuing higher education at the time of this writing. When they were growing up, I went to great pains to make sure my boys were fed, clothed, housed, educated, and loved. If a normal man like me would take such great care of his sons, can we not believe that God would take even better care of his children? Luke 11:13 reads, "If you then, though you are evil, know how to give good gifts to your children, how much more will your Father in heaven give the Holy Spirit to those who ask him!"

God's response to our prayers is consistent with his nature. God is good, loves people and wants the best for them. His gift of the Holy Spirit is evidence that God responds to prayer out of his goodness. Luke indicates that the Holy Spirit is the best gift God could give his children. Christians receive this gift at the time of their salvation.

The Holy Spirit works with us as we pray consistently. The Spirit keeps us from giving up when things are rough. For example, Luther Rice lived from 1783 until 1836. He was a single man who was appointed as a missionary to India by the American Board of Commissioners for Foreign Missions, an interdenominational group. Rice became a Baptist in 1812 and was denied support. He returned to the United States to raise the funds he and Adoniram and Ann Judson needed for the work in India. Rice never returned to the mission fields in India. Instead he traveled extensively promoting mission causes within the Triennial Convention, the first general association of Baptists in the United States. Persistent prayer characterized Luther Rice's life. The Spirit of God helped him in his travels and work on behalf of missions. He accepted God's invitation to pray.

Medical doctor and researcher Herbert Bensen says, "[H]umans are, in a profound physical way, 'wired for God.'"[13] Bensen notes that we come into the world with hard-wired instincts, such as fear of heights and fear of snakes. These are genetically predisposed patterns of behavior. He writes that his discovery of this idea came to him suddenly:

[M]y interactions with patients, their families, and with people in general led me to believe that my hypothesis was sound. The idea that humans are wired for God, that we are custom-made to engage in and exercise beliefs, and that spiritual beliefs are the most powerful of that sort, felt like a truth that had always existed inside of me and inside of humankind to which I had suddenly gained conscious access.[14]

Our physically based need to interact with God is powerful, as Bensen writes:

Religious groups encourage all kinds of health-affirming activities, fellowship and socializing perhaps first among them, but also prayer, volunteerism, familiar rituals, and music. Prayer, in particular, appears to be therapeutic, the specifics of which science will continue to explore.[15]

Bensen's research observations affirm what the Bible has already said in many different ways. We have a need to reach out to God. Why? Because God has already reached out to us. That may be the physically based situation that Bensen calls being "wired for God."

We do not want to say that prayer is only based on our physical makeup, however. We do not want to say that prayer is "only" any one thing. Something as complex as communication between God and mankind can never be "only" any one simple thing. Some things seem completely inadequate if we squeeze them too hard. We cannot shrink things to an irreducible minimum without losing the essence. George Buttrick says that sometimes this process goes too far. He uses this example: "Science defines a tear as 'a drop of saline liquid secreted by the lachrymal gland, ordinarily conveyed away by the lachrymal canal to the lachrymal sac, whence it passes into the meatus of the nose and mingles with the mucous secretion.'"[16] True, but is that really a tear? Does that describe what moistens our face at a funeral? Can that adequately capture the emotional release at our wedding or the birth of our children?

For many complex reasons we have a strong need to reach out to God. I visited the site of the federal building in Oklahoma City one year after it was bombed. The area was fenced off, and hundreds of items, such as messages and toys and plaques, were tied onto the fence. Over one hundred other people were there at the same time I was, and nearly everyone was silent. A woman standing next to me had a young daughter who looked to be about four or five years old. The girl kept talking. Finally the mother said, "Honey, you have to be quiet here. This is a sacred place."

What did she mean by that? Why was it sacred? Wasn't it because the enormity of what had happened there brought home our human mortality? Somehow that place reminded people of eternal things. It called people to consider the deeper issues of life and death. It called people to pray. You, too, are invited to pray. Will you answer that call?

It's Your Turn Now

We began this chapter with your reading an invitation from the Lord. How will you answer it? Here are several things you might want to consider as you learn to pray.

- You might gather a group and plan a prayer retreat in which you plan strategies to develop a lifestyle of prayer.
- You might commit yourself to spend a significant amount of time in prayer each week.
- You might choose prayer partners as a way of encouraging each other in your prayer lives.
- You might develop some sort of prayer calendar or journal in which you log your needs, petitions, and answers received.

God's invitation to pray is real. RSVP.

Questions for Further Reflection

1. Do you think scripture really gives an invitation to pray?
2. Jesus' first disciples asked, "Lord, teach us to pray." If you could ask Jesus something about prayer, what would it be?
3. Why do you think Jesus made a lifelong habit of prayer?
4. Is there an area of your life in which you need to "ask, seek, and knock"?
5. Recall the story of the philosopher and his would-be disciple. What do you really want out of your relationship with God?
6. David Whyte contends, "the conversation *is* the relationship." How does that pertain to prayer?
7. Reflect on the phrase "fierce conversation." What does that mean in relationship to God?

2

A Stubborn Misunderstanding of Prayer

"And when you pray, do not be like the hypocrites, for they love to pray standing in the synagogues and on the street corners to be seen by men. I tell you the truth, they have received their reward in full. But when you pray, go into your room, close the door and pray to your Father, who is unseen. Then your Father, who sees what is done in secret, will reward you. And when you pray, do not keep on babbling like pagans, for they think they will be heard because of their many words. Do not be like them, for your Father knows what you need before you ask him."

MATTHEW 6:5–8

What does the word *prayer* bring to your mind? A regular meeting at church? A last-ditch effort to stave off some disaster? An intimate communication between you and God? All of these images, or others, might come to mind when we think of prayer.

A ball game is about to begin. Silence is called for and someone begins to intone words of protection for the players. Is that prayer? A soldier in a battle raises his eyes to heaven in a silent plea for protection. Is that prayer? A woman kneels on a bench in a church building and begins to commune with God in a way that seems more like a dialogue than a monologue. Is that prayer? A young person faces an important test so she fingers the cross hanging around her neck. Is that prayer? As is obvious in just these few images, prayer has many facets. George Appleton concurs:

> The word "prayer" embraces a number of meanings and covers a number of activities. In its most elementary form it is asking God for the things we need, material or spiritual. It can be thanksgiving for what God has done for us; it can be worship of God for what he is. It can be fellowship with God, enjoying our touch with him, quiet reflection in his presence. It can be the expression of our concern for people or for what is happening in the world and in the Church. It can be vocal, when we express ourselves in words, or it can be silent and contemplative, resting in his presence, the sphere of the timeless and the eternal. Prayer is as essential to the inner life as breath is to the body.[1]

Prayer, as we see above, can be many things and comes in many forms. But not all ideas about prayer are biblically correct. We will be considering many ideas about prayer in this small book. But sometimes we can tell what a thing is by discovering what it is *not.* This is true with prayer. If, at the very beginning of our study, we explore several popular ideas that are probably wrong, then we will be on our way toward discovering what prayer really is. Let me point out something here, though. These ideas about prayer are stubborn and keep cropping up in every generation. One major reason for this fact is that they are immature notions. New Christians especially are prone to believe these ideas. Often, when a person has a chance to grow and mature in relationship to Christ, prayer will take on a deeper meaning.

Prayer Is Not a Lottery

A lottery is a game of chance. A person gambles that what he bets will reward his efforts by paying off more than the original bet. I do not mean to sound crass when I suggest that some people seem to think of prayer in this lottery fashion. They think,

"Hey, I'll say a prayer in this situation. It couldn't hurt anything, and it might pay off big."

This way of thinking is purely selfish. The sole motive behind the act is to gamble that a few words mumbled to the deity might "do some good." As you read the Bible you will find many prayers addressed to God. People who were in trouble said many of those prayers. They asked for help. The difference between those instances and the contemporary prayer-as-lottery view is this: the people in the Bible who prayed for help generally already had a relationship with God established. They were asking the help of the One whom they knew as the Lord. They were not just casting out verbiage in the hopes that it might possibly be heard by "the man upstairs" and answered affirmatively.

Prayer Is Not a Twist of God's Arm

Another popular notion about prayer is that it is a way to make God do something he does not want to do. It is a way to twist God's arm to force him to do your will. Most people would never state the case so boldly and probably most would even deny that is what they believe. However, when you hear what some people pray for, and the way they ask for it, you realize that they are trying to force their will on God.

But doesn't the Bible have examples of this? Aren't some situations in the Bible exactly that? Consider the example of Jesus, who cursed a fig tree. On what we call Palm Sunday Jesus entered Jerusalem, but then went back to Bethany to spend the night. The next morning, on Monday, he and the disciples were on their way back to Jerusalem when Jesus spotted a fig tree in full leaf. He went up to it expecting to find it as full of fruit as it was full of green leaves. He found nothing, however. Mark 11:14 says, "Then he said to the tree, 'May no one ever eat fruit from you again.' And his disciples heard him say it." The next day, Tuesday morning, Jesus and the twelve were again going to Jerusalem. They saw that the tree had withered overnight. Simon Peter said, "Rabbi, look! The fig tree you cursed has withered!" (11:21b).

This story causes some modern people trouble because of a misunderstanding of the concept of curse in the Bible. A curse

was not what we today would call a "four-letter word." It was
not a "nasty" reference. A good curse was earthy, specific, and a
call to action. It might be something like these two: "May the
fleas of a thousand camels infest your armpits," and, "May all
your teeth fall out but one, and in that one may you get a
toothache." In cursing the fig tree, Jesus was calling for action on
the part of his disciples and using it as an object lesson or
prophetic symbolism.

Mark ties this story with the cleansing of the temple. A fig
tree with no fruit was exactly like the temple, which produced
no fruit. The cursing of the tree was a prophetic sign. The fig
tree's leaves promised fruit, but the tree bore no fruit. The tree's
appearance was deceptive. It stood as a symbol of what Jesus
had found in the temple. It, too, looked promising. The temple
had a long history and promised seekers that they could find a
place of worship, a place that would help them find God. What
they found was chaos like the day after Christmas at a store or
mall. To this farce Jesus raised his whip and his voice and said in
effect, "Enough! You shall not make my Father's house a place
of empty promises in which you are more interested in revenue
than reverence."

Jesus' action was in line with the Old Testament prophets.
He saw the leaders of the temple as being like the one described
in Jeremiah 8:13: "When I wanted to gather them, says the
LORD, there are no grapes on the vine, nor figs on the fig tree;
even the leaves are withered, and what I gave them has passed
away from them" (NRSV). Bible scholar Richard Gardner notes
that this action is symbolic. He wrote, "Jesus' action, then, signifies
the judgment of God on a religious community that 'is covered
with the ostentatious foliage of external piety,' but in which 'truly
obedient deeds, the fruit of religion, are lacking...'"[2] Jesus,
quoting from Isaiah 56:7 and Jeremiah 7:11, said, "'My house
will be called a house of prayer...,' / but you have made it 'a
den of robbers.'"

Jesus called for action with his curse. It may have been a
form of prayer in that he used it to accomplish God's will. He
was not simply being spiteful, nor was he lashing out from hurt
pride. The key is that Jesus did not try to make God do something
that God was unwilling to do. Jesus worked in harmony with the

will of God and not against it.³ That fact is central when we
think about prayer. We pray to lay hold of God's willingness, not
to make God do our will.

Prayer Is Not an Automatic Guarantee of Success

A subtle misunderstanding of prayer is to think of it as a
guarantee of success. Someone might think, "I really need to get
an edge. I'll ask God to help me win." Now we certainly want to
pray in all things, but to imagine that prayer will give us a
guarantee of success is immature. So how do we pray for things
like our jobs and decisions we need to make? What good does
prayer do in these situations? Consider the example of John
Marks Templeton.

Templeton is the founder of the successful Templeton Mutual
Fund Group. He is regarded as one of Wall Street's wisest
investors. Many years ago he committed himself to Christ and
became a man of prayer. He began to open all of the directors'
and shareholders' meetings with prayer. But he points out that
prayer is never used as a tool in making specific stock selections:

> That would be a gross misinterpretation of God's meth-
> ods. What we do pray for is wisdom. We pray that the
> decisions we make today will be wise decisions and that
> our talks about different stocks will be wise talks. Of
> course, our discussions and decisions are fallible and
> sometimes flawed. No one should expect that, just
> because he begins with prayer, every decision he makes
> is going to be profitable.⁴

He continues, "However, I do believe that, if you pray, you
will make fewer stupid mistakes."

This is true in other areas of life and not just in business. I
know a young woman who worked for a Christian organization.
She became extremely ill. Her colleagues prayed for her and
assured her she would recover. Instead her condition worsened.
She wanted to seek medical attention but her colleagues told
her that if she just had enough faith and prayed more she would
get well. Finally her condition deteriorated to the point she simply
had to get medical help. He doctor discovered she had colon
cancer, a potentially deadly diagnosis. She had surgery to remove

part of her colon and had to undergo chemotherapy. All the while her colleagues were disappointed that she "didn't have enough faith." Ultimately she left that company and found a job elsewhere where people did not try to use God and guilt to achieve what they wanted. Prayer is no substitute for hard work and personal responsibility. It helps us make decisions and work smarter, but it is not an automatic guarantee of success.

Prayer Is Not Meaningless Ritual

My family has prayer at meal times. My wife and I have done this since we first married, and we have taught our children to say grace at the table. This ritual is important to us and it expresses our daily gratitude for our food. Many people say a prayer at meal times, or before bed, or at a ball game. The saying of the prayers might be meaningful, or it might just be a ritual performed at stated times simply because you have always done it.

We need to remember that such rituals can be important but they might seem strange to those who do not understand them. During the early days of our nation, a traveling preacher went to a frontier town to hold religious services. The town had received very little religious influence before the preacher's arrival. He stayed with a family in town who had a little boy. On the first evening of his arrival everyone gathered around the table for supper. The preacher bowed his head and said an audible prayer. The little boy had never seen anything like that before. The child saw the preacher on the street the next day and asked, "Are you the fellow who talks to his plate?"[5]

A contemporary musician posted the following information on a public Internet forum. He was referring to the fact that he was battling cancer:

> At the present time I am in a hospice setting for a number of tests to figure out what's going on with the prostate cancer I've had since 1998. Been here for a week. It seems to be a number of non-operable metastasis [*sic*] to my lymph nodes. I am awaiting the test results. I SHOULD be home by the end of the week.

I am NOT a religious person in the Christian sense of the word, and I would strongly resent anyone laying THEIR trip on me. Suffice to say, I do have my own quite strong belief system concerning issues of man, his place in the universe, his relation to God, and the immortality of the soul. I would simply ask for those on the list to send good thoughts my way in whatever way they find appropriate but to please spare me any preaching. It is a real rough patch and I'd like all the help I can get."[6]

Shortly after that posting he lost his fight with cancer. What interests me about his message is that even though he described himself in nontraditional religious terms, and did not want anyone trying to squeeze him into their faith ideas, still he wanted people to remember him in some way. Sending "good thoughts" may be how he described prayer and "all the help" he could get. He apparently thought the effort to remember him in this way was not an empty religious ritual.

Prayer Is Not a Purely Personal Religious Act with No Social Consequences

Praying is one of the most intimate things a person can do. To reach out to the God of creation with words and feelings is a tremendously personal act. Some people have described religion in general—and prayer in particular—with reference to this privacy. I have read definitions such as, "Religion is what one does with his solitude." I am not sure what that means, because there are many things we can do with our solitude. Such a definition tries to paint religion and prayer as nothing more than purely private communication between a person and God.

The problem with that definition is that it stops too soon. Prayer is personal and intimate, but it is not purely private. One of the overwhelming teachings in the Bible about prayer is that prayer moves us from our selfish preoccupations to something beyond ourselves. The letter of James in the New Testament has this passage: "What good is it, my brothers, if a man claims to have faith but has no deeds? Can such faith save him? Suppose a brother or sister is without clothes and daily food. If one of you says to him, 'Go, I wish you well; keep warm and well fed,' but does nothing about his physical needs, what good is it? In the same way, faith by itself, if it is not accompanied by action, is dead" (2:14–17). Prayer, in other words, should move us not only toward God, but also toward our fellow humans.

Frederick Douglass was a slave who became a freedman. His autobiography was first published in 1845. He told of the conditions under which he had lived before being freed:

> There were four slaves of us in the kitchen—my sister Eliza, my aunt Priscilla, Henry, and myself; and we were allowed less than a half a bushel of corn-meal per week, and very little else, either in the shape of meat or vegetables. It was not enough for us to subsist upon. We were therefore reduced to the wretched necessity of living at the expense of our neighbors. This we did by begging and stealing, whichever came handy in the time of need, the one being considered as legitimate as the other. A great many times have we poor creatures been nearly perishing with hunger, when food in abundance lay smouldering in the safe and smoke-house, and our pious mistress was aware of the fact; and yet that mistress and her husband would kneel every morning, and pray that God would bless them in basket and store![7]

How does that stack up against the instruction of James?

How many people will go hungry tonight while praying for something to eat tomorrow? Is their effort just empty words poured out into an uncaring universe?

Prayer Is Not Getting in Touch with Mystical Powers

We live in an age of generic spirituality. We often hear about spiritual values, but by that term many people mean inner personal values rather than a reference to God. A term that is often associated with spirituality today is "New Age." That is something of a catchall term that lumps all religious, metaphysical, and spiritual quests into the same category. It might include channeling, Tarot cards, belief in reincarnation, and other such manifestations. So what is prayer in New Age philosophy? It is the attempt to get in touch with the mystical forces of the universe and to influence those forces. That is done through repeating a mantra—a special word or phrase—or by deeply meditating. The attempt to influence the powers of the universe traditionally has been called magic.

C. S. Lewis, the well-known writer from England who has influenced so many, was especially careful not to allow prayer to sink to the level of seeming to be magic. He wrote, "The very question 'Does prayer work?' puts us in the wrong frame of mind from the outset. 'Work': as if it were magic, or a machine— something that functions automatically."[8] His point is that prayer is communication between God and mankind, not a scientific formula in which everything is certain. Nor is prayer an "open-sesame" guarantee to open the doors of heaven. Again, that concept is magic.

Magic is defined this way:

1. The art that purports to control or forecast natural events, effects, or forces by invoking the supernatural.
2. The practice of using charms, spells, or rituals to attempt to produce supernatural effects or to control events in nature.[9]

Christian prayer is different from all this because it seeks to get in touch with not a what but a Whom. In other words, prayer reaches out to God as a loving Heavenly Father who wants the best for his children rather than to a mysterious, capricious force of nature. Prayer is thus personal communication that moves beyond the "gimme" aspect of life to communion with the Holy God. One person wrote, "The big watershed is moving from trying to control God to letting God direct me."[10]

I once flew from New Orleans to Kansas City. The flight stopped in St. Louis, where I was supposed to change planes and continue to my destination. When I tried to find the flight number, I discovered that it had been canceled weeks before but the travel agent never told me. For a few minutes I felt trapped, but then I took a deep breath and went to talk to the airline personnel. They found me a flight with another company and had me on my way with only a slight delay. That company was moving their plane to Kansas City so my new flight had only three passengers on it! The stewardess told me they needed to balance the plane and asked if I would mind sitting in first class. I went from having no transportation—a canceled flight—to going first class. All I had to do was let someone know my need.

That experience reminds me that God's intentions for us include our overall well-being. I am not saying that simply asking God for everything we want is a guaranteed way to get it. Instead, we answer the invitation to learn to pray and live with the awareness that God is with us and has our best interests at heart. C. S. Lewis once spoke of our confusing sense of need:

> Our Lord finds our desires, not too strong, but too weak. We are half-hearted creatures, fooling about with drink and sex and ambition when infinite joy is offered us, like an ignorant child who wants to go on making mud pies in a slum because he cannot imagine what is meant by the offer of a holiday at the sea. We are far too easily pleased.[11]

Learn to avoid some of the stubborn misunderstandings about prayer. Learn to pray in all areas of life and do not be too easily satisfied. I personally want to help the kingdom of God grow instead of making mud pies in the slum. How about you?

It's Your Turn Now

All these things, then, tell us a little about what prayer is *not:*

- Prayer is not a lottery.
- Prayer is not a twisting of God's arm to make him do what we want.
- Prayer is not an automatic guarantee of success.
- Prayer is not a meaningless ritual. Nor is prayer merely a private act with no consequences.
- Prayer is not getting in touch with the mystical forces of the universe.

Prayer *is* communicating with God, the Creator and Sustainer of all life. No wonder prayer is misunderstood. But it is too important to be left to chance. Think of some ways to put into effect what you learned in this chapter. Examine your previous understanding (or misunderstanding) of prayer. Notice anything that needs to change?

Questions for Reflection and Discussion

1. What do you usually think of when you hear the word *prayer*?
2. Can you list other things or ideas that prayer is *not*?
3. Can prayer be a guarantee of success in any endeavor?
4. What are some ways that people try to make God do what they want him to do?
5. What are some of the social consequences that might be associated with prayer?
6. What is prayer in New Age religious expressions?
7. What do you make of C. S. Lewis's comment about making mud pies in the slum?
8. What is the most important insight you learned from this chapter?

3

Pray Like This

"Be careful not to do your 'acts of righteousness' before men, to be seen by them. If you do, you will have no reward from your Father in heaven.

"So when you give to the needy, do not announce it with trumpets, as the hypocrites do in the synagogues and on the streets, to be honored by men. I tell you the truth, they have received their reward in full. But when you give to the needy, do not let your left hand know what your right hand is doing, so that your giving may be in secret. Then your Father, who sees what is done in secret, will reward you...

"For if you forgive men when they sin against you, your heavenly Father will also forgive you. But if you do not forgive men their sins, your Father will not forgive your sins."

MATTHEW 6:1–4; 14–15

A young man asked, "Pastor, how should I pray? I've read a book or two on the subject, but I'm still not sure just what it is I'm supposed to do." He was completely serious in his request. The pastor wisely guided the young man to examine Matthew 6 for guidelines in prayer. This is a teaching selection from Jesus himself. If anyone can help us learn to pray, he can. Matthew 6 also includes the "Lord's Prayer," Jesus' model for personal prayer.

Getting Our Motives Right

Prayer, like most religious acts, is best done for the benefit of God and his reign. Our prayers are not to be said just so other people will hear us pray and think, "Gee, that person certainly is religious." Prayer is deep personal communication between you and God. When it becomes a show or performance, it ceases to be prayer.

Jesus warned against publicity hunting—doing religiously showy things for people to see. When someone does something for show, the praise he or she gets from other people is the entire reward. There is nothing else. God considers the praises as "paid in full."

A person who used to be on a nationally televised religious program stated that the only time she and her husband ever prayed was on television! They never prayed together at home.[1] God does not hear prayers that are said only to be seen by others.

Jesus warned against wordiness. The pagans, he said, use many words in their prayers. Perhaps they thought that by multiplying words they could somehow make God listen. Jesus knew we cannot force God to do anything.

We certainly live in a day of wordiness. Some people try to use fancy words to say things that could easily be stated more simply, or they try to take the bite out of potentially troubling problems by concealing them in deliberately convoluted language. This evasion of unpleasantness is called doublespeak. Consider these examples of what I mean:

- A gas company no longer sends a gas bill; now it is called an "energy document."
- An auto company laid off 5000 workers; they called the layoff a "career alternative enhancement program."
- A recent medical publication warned that jumping off a building could result in "sudden deceleration trauma" upon landing.
- The military no longer says it is going to war; it now engages in "lethal intervention," which could result in "excess mortality."

- Even common devices are subject to becoming other things: a zipper is an "interlocking slide fastener"; a toothbrush is a "home plaque removal instrument."

Prayer is not religious doublespeak. It is deep, committed communication between an individual or groups and God. This fact helps ensure that prayer is offered from the right motives as Jesus taught them.

Getting the Model Right

A friend of mine owns a small mobile home refurbishing business. He once found a crumpled up piece of paper in one of the trailers and gave it to me. The handwritten note contains a "formula" for praying. This is what is scrawled on that note:

Get 3 glasses of water at 12 o'clock; pray 3 Our Father prayers, pray 3 23rd Psalms. Set all 3 glasses on refrigerator at 5 AM in the morning. Go to front door. Say, "In the name of the Father, in the name of the Son, in the name of the Holy Ghost." Follow Thursday. Follow Friday. Get all bills, place on a white plate; take your right hand and place over bills. Pray like you never prayed before; offer bills each up to God. Set plate on top of refrigerator; lay your Bible on 23rd Psalms; take out as you can pay each bill.

Did this formula for prayer work? I guess not. This paper was found in a repossessed trailer!

Jesus did offer a model for his followers to use in praying—the Lord's Prayer. It is not some magic formula to success, but it is a guide to know what God will listen and respond to. Let us examine the various parts of the prayer.

The Lord's Prayer as it appears in Matthew 6:9–13 is broken down and discussed in detail below. To begin, verses 9 and 10 pertain to God's rule over people and their honoring him as their Lord.

"Our Father"

Jesus spoke in Aramaic, a language similar to Hebrew. He spoke of God as *Abba,* which is a personal term similar to our term "Daddy." This term expresses our relationship to God and his nature. God is not only the Eternal Lord of the universe; he is also the Father of Jesus and of his followers. Theological scholar Fisher Humphreys has noted:

> Abba is a term which speaks of God's friendliness and love, as well as of His parental authority; it suggests that the disciples are children who love and trust God and who try to be obedient to Him.[2]

This is a personal term of address. Christians may reach out to God with the realization that he is our Heavenly Father who cares for us. Because of that fact we reach out in the most intimate of ways—as a child to a parent. Richard Foster says, "God receives us just as we are and accepts our prayers just as they are. In the same way that a small child cannot draw a bad picture so a child of God cannot offer a bad prayer."[3]

"In heaven"

While the term *Father* suggests that God is close and personal, the phrase "in heaven" reminds us that God is not just a good buddy next door. He is above and beyond us. God is not earthbound or temporary. He is heavenly and everlasting. He is transcendent.

"Hallowed be your name"

This part of Jesus' model prayer teaches us that God's name is separate from all other names. It is holy, which is the meaning of the word *hallowed*. In the Bible, someone's name referred to that person's whole character. God's name is hallowed when his nature and purpose are known and reverenced. People should show reverence for God.

"Your kingdom come"

God's kingdom is his rule in the hearts and lives of his people. To pray this part of the prayer is to pledge yourself to join God's effort to extend his rule to everyone. This prayer is sincere when we want others to know the lordship of God.

"Your will be done on earth as it is in heaven"

This is a request that God's purpose be carried out among persons. What is his purpose? Humphreys has written the following:

God's purpose is to create a worldwide family of persons
who freely accept God as their God and who receive his
love into their lives, and who respond to him by loving
him with all their hearts and loving their neighbors as
themselves.[4]

This, in a very succinct manner, is what God wills. When
we pray, "Your will be done," we are saying, "Lord, I want what
you will for me. I pledge to work for your purpose in life."

"Give us today our daily bread"

God's care for his children includes their total welfare. The
needs of the body are important, as are the needs of the soul.
Jesus taught that God is interested in our everyday needs. This
includes food, certainly, but I think it includes all of our basic
needs.

We may properly pray for *all* matters in our daily lives. These
could include our home, our job, our health, our relationships
with other people, and our deepest physical and emotional needs.
Jesus taught that we can pray about everything that makes up
daily life. I take that to mean that God invites our prayers
regarding our hurts, our hang-ups, our sexual desires, our
loneliness, and anything else we may wish to share with him
and have him assist us with. In short, we may rightly pray about
everything that touches our lives.

I had to have surgery several years ago to correct a defect in
my skull due to an earlier accident. The surgery went well, but
while in recovery I began throwing up so much that my heart
went into an irregular rhythm. That was on a Wednesday. The
doctors told me the next day that they were going to sedate me
and place a tube down my throat to examine my heart. If it was
healthy, they were going to shock it back into rhythm the day
after that, Friday.

That evening as I thought about all that I had been through
and what was to come next, I felt the strongest urge to pray
specifically about my health. I had been doing so all along but
the feeling was to be as specific as possible. I began praying that
my heart would go back into regular rhythm and that the
procedure for shocking it would be unnecessary. After praying

for some time, I relaxed and went to sleep at 11:00 p.m. I awoke about 4:00 a.m. Thursday and knew immediately that my heart was beating normally. Part of my "daily bread" was the desire to be well again and I felt completely free to pray about what I needed most. God graciously granted it.

This part of our prayer lives need not be long and cumbersome. A Washington lawyer once got hold of this section of the model prayer and it ended up like this:

> We respectively petition, request, and entreat that due and adequate provision be made, this day and the date hereinafter subscribed, for the organizing of such methods of allocation and distribution as may be deemed necessary and proper to assure the reception by and for said petitioners of such quantities of baked cereal products as shall, in the judgment of the aforesaid petitioners, constitute a sufficient supply thereof.[5]

I wonder what the whole prayer might look like!

C. S. Lewis pondered the mystery of Jesus' teaching people to pray like this:

> Petitionary prayer is…both allowed and commanded to us: "Give us our daily bread." And no doubt it raises a theoretical problem. Can we believe that God ever really modifies His action in response to the suggestions of men? For infinite wisdom does not need telling what is best, and infinite goodness needs no urging to do it. But neither does God need any of those things that are done by his finite agents, whether living or inanimate. He could, if He chose, repair our bodies miraculously without food; or give us good without the aid of farmers, bakers, or butchers; or knowledge without the aid of learned men; or convert the heathen without missionaries. Instead, He allows soils and weather and animals and the muscles, minds, and wills of men to cooperate with His will.[6]

In God's grace, our prayers matter to God! Things happen when people pray. "God," said Blaise Pascal, a seventeenth-century philosopher, "instituted prayer in order to lend to His creatures the dignity of causality."[7] Our prayers matter.

"Forgive us our debts, as we also have forgiven our debtors"

More will be said about forgiveness below. For now we can simply note that Jesus made this a matter of importance. Forgiveness opens the door to relationships, both with God and with other people.

"And lead us not into temptation, but deliver us from the evil one"

This part of Jesus' prayer has troubled many people. Does God actually tempt us? The word translated as "temptation" is, in the original language, *peirasmos.* It can mean both "temptation" and "trial." God does not "tempt" people with evil enticement. James 1:13 says, "When tempted, no one should say, 'God is tempting me.' For God cannot be tempted by evil, nor does he tempt anyone…"

I think that Jesus meant that we should pray about the trials that come in our lives. His phrase "lead us not into temptation" means "do not let us fall into a trial so difficult that we will fail."[8] The issue is testing.

Booker T. Washington tells in his autobiography, *Up from Slavery,* about the children of his white masters. They were pampered and never taught specific skills. The slaves, though, were taught how to work. After the Civil War, many of the white children who had never learned to work were in trouble because they did not know how to do anything. Most black people knew how to work and could at least make a living. Trials came for both. Some stood up well under the testing while others did not.[9]

The individual petitions in Jesus' model prayer end here. The next section is a summary of what needs to be done to keep the door of communication open.

Getting the Attitude Right

Forgiveness is spiritual nourishment that renews the mind and spirit the way food renews the body. It is a two-way street that carries the traffic of incoming hurt and outgoing pain. Individuals can and should reach out to others and invite them to come close. Forgiveness is thus an open door through which we invite other people to be our neighbors.

Jesus concluded his model prayer with these words: "For if you forgive men when they sin against you, your heavenly Father will also forgive you. But if you do not forgive men their sins, your Father will not forgive your sins" (Mt. 6:14–15). These are strong and straightforward words. Make no mistake. Genuine forgiveness is not easy! A library says it "forgives" fines, but that is not really forgiveness. Genuine forgiveness is costly to all involved. It cost God the life of his Son to forgive us. It costs our pride and rebellion to accept it. Forgiveness between people is equally costly because we must open the door to people who have betrayed or hurt us. That is not easy.

The alternative—not to forgive—is even worse. "If you do not forgive men their sins, your Father will not forgive your sins." It is that simple, and that difficult.

Prayer is too important to misunderstand or to leave to chance. After all, prayer is getting in touch with the Lord of all creation, all time, and all space. What could compare with that?

But let's face this fact: Many people have great questions about prayer and think of it as nonsense. Winston Churchill was such a man, at least for a while. In his autobiography, he recalled his early life, which included rebelling against the idea of faith and prayer. Consider what he said about himself:

> I passed through a violent and aggressive anti-religious phase, which, had it lasted, might easily have made me a nuisance. My poise was restored during the next few years by frequent contact with danger. I found that whatever I might think and argue, I did not hesitate to ask for special protection when about to come under the fire of the enemy; nor to feel sincerely grateful when I got home safe to tea. I even asked for lesser things than not to be killed too soon, and nearly in these years…I got what I wanted. This practice [of prayer] seemed perfectly natural, and just as strong and real as the reasoning process which contradicted it so sharply.[10]

We may never face situations such as those Churchill did, but we will face our share of crises. Knowing God through prayer will get us through those tough times.

It's Your Turn Now

• Why not use this week as a time of taking to heart the meaning of Jesus' prayer?
• You might memorize the Lord's Prayer.
• You might use the individual sections of the Lord's Prayer for your prayer time. For example, on Monday you might spend time thinking about the meaning of the phrase, "Our Father," and then pray to your heavenly Father. On Tuesday you might think about the phrase "in heaven," and so on.

Questions for Further Reflection

1. Why is the prayer Jesus taught called the "model prayer"?
2. What did you learn in this chapter about the various parts of the prayer?
3. Is there anything you think you should *not* pray for? If so, what?
4. Think about the author's experience in the hospital and his specific prayer. Is there something that specific that calls forth your prayer?
5. Reflect on the words of Winston Churchill. Can you identify with some of his thoughts?

4

Your Attitude Is Important

Then Jesus told his disciples a parable to show them that they should always pray and not give up. He said: "In a certain town there was a judge who neither feared God nor cared about men. And there was a widow in that town who kept coming to him with the plea, 'Grant me justice against my adversary.'

"For some time he refused. But finally he said to himself, 'Even though I don't fear God or care about men, yet because this widow keeps bothering me, I will see that she gets justice, so that she won't eventually wear me out with her coming!'"

And the Lord said, "Listen to what the unjust judge says. And will not God bring about justice for his chosen ones, who cry out to him day and night? Will he keep putting them off? I tell you, he will see that they get justice, and quickly. However, when the Son of Man comes, will he find faith on the earth?"

To some who were confident of their own righteousness and looked down on everybody else, Jesus told this parable: "Two men went up to the temple to pray, one a Pharisee and the other a tax collector. The Pharisee stood up and prayed about himself; 'God, I thank you that I am not like all other men—robbers, evildoers, adulterers—or even like this tax collector. I fast twice a week and give a tenth of all I get.'

"But the tax collector stood at a distance. He would not even look up to heaven, but beat his breast and said, 'God, have mercy on me, a sinner.'
"I tell you that this man, rather than the other, went home justified before God. For everyone who exalts himself will be humbled, and he who humbles himself will be exalted."

LUKE 18:1–14

"Do you believe in prayer?" These words spun in my brain as I answered the phone at 3:00 a.m. The anonymous caller had gotten my name out of the directory and phoned one morning to see if prayer mattered. When the grogginess wore off and I woke up, I questioned the caller about what he meant. He said, "I'm lonesome and I want you to pray that God would send me a wife." I asked him to repeat the request so I could be sure I was not dreaming. He again asked me to pray that God would send him a wife—soon!

We talked on for a few minutes and I became convinced that he was serious. I began to explain that prayer is not a vending machine in which we automatically get what we want, but my early-morning caller would have none of my explanations. He said just before he hung up, "Look, either prayer works or it doesn't. It's that simple. Now are you going to pray what I asked you for or not?"

I did pray and ask God that this young man could meet a girl, form a deep and lasting relationship, and get married. What I did not do, however, was to request that the Lord send him a wife in the manner that J. C. Penney sends me a package when I order from their catalogue.

What attitude should we have when we pray? This is an important question.

Pray with Perseverance

Jesus, the greatest of all teachers, often used simple stories to communicate his message. Stories and parables have a way of getting around people's defenses and going deep into their lives. Verses 1–7 of Luke 18 form a parable on prayer. Its purpose is spelled out in verse 1—"that they should always pray and not give up."

Anyone who has been a Christian for very long and has done much praying knows that discouragement can sometimes set in. We lift our voices to God, but seemingly get nothing but silence. Jesus knew that this was the situation, so he taught the disciples to pray in such a manner that they would expect delays. The delays in the answer do not mean that God does not hear, however. Jesus told the disciples that they must never give up as they prayed and worked. Christians can overcome possible discouragement by continuing to pray, no matter what.

The woman in the parable faced what seemed to be an immovable obstacle—a judge who did not care about justice! He thought of himself as the last word in all matters because he "neither feared God nor cared about men" (v. 2b). What happens when a Christian runs up against a brick wall? Do you just stay there? Run? Hide? Back up and hit it again?

Jesus' parable demonstrates that the widow had the kind of attitude needed to succeed in prayer. She would not take "no" for an answer. Her example shows us that perseverance in prayer is characterized by continual, constant praying. Because her need was desperate, the woman kept on asking.

The attitude of seriousness and tenacity is an essential part of the Christian life in general and of prayer in particular. If we approach a problem with the right attitude, we may not get instant results, but neither will we get discouraged.

Can anything lasting and worthwhile be gotten with little effort and in a short time? A career takes a long time to establish. A relationship takes time and effort to develop. The same is true with prayer. The more we pray, the better able we are to pray. We become more comfortable with this way of expressing ourselves. We also become better able to hear God as he answers us. Even when the answer seems to be silence, we can endure it through persistence.

The judge in the parable decided to act on the widow's behalf, not because he wanted to serve justice, but because he wanted to get rid of this nuisance! (At least, that is what he considered her.) The focal point of the parable is on the widow's attitude, not on the judge's attitude.

To the judge, power, justice, and authority were commodities to be bought and sold like so much merchandise. The woman had no cash, no social standing, and no power. All she had was a need and a desire to get something done. She hounded the judge day and night until he got tired of her. The old proverb says, "The squeaky wheel gets the grease." In this case, the persistent widow got her desire. The judge reasoned, "because this widow keeps bothering me, I will see that she gets justice, so that she won't eventually wear me out with her coming" (v. 5).

If a persistent widow can gain justice from a callous judge, will not a child of God get what he or she needs from God by asking? That is the point of the story. If even a crooked judge can be moved to action by persistence, then certainly a loving heavenly Father will be moved even more by the persistent prayers of his children.

Verses 6 and 7 indicate that God is ready and willing to hear us. "And the Lord said, 'Listen to what the unjust judge says. And will not God bring about justice for his chosen ones, who cry out to him day and night? Will he keep putting them off?'"

Let me give a personal illustration of this principle. I once lived in a nice house that we bought in 1989. It has four bedrooms and sits on two acres of land. It was just right for our needs. When we were looking for a house we looked at many but could not find anything we really wanted. When we found this one, my wife and I both said, "Yes," immediately. When we went to the mortgage company for a loan, they assured us there would be no problem and that we could close within four weeks. Everything went wrong after that! The loan was supposed to be assumable, but the assumption on the loan was not what the owner had said it was so we turned it down. That meant we had to start from scratch with a new loan. That took another two months because of the incompetence of the mortgage company.

All the while friends kept asking us, "Are you sure you want that house? Maybe the Lord is trying to tell you something." Their assumption seems to have been that since there were problems, perhaps the Lord did not want us to have this house. We kept praying and feeling that he did want us to have it. So we toughed it out and kept pressing the mortgage company to finish the work. Finally, over three months after we first agreed to buy the house, we moved in.

Just because events do not flow smoothly, do not assume that God is not in those events. The life of faith is a rocky and rough trail, not a six-lane superhighway. Jesus said to pray your way through these difficulties and tough spots.

British writer Samuel Johnson, once wrote:

> All the performances of human art, at which we look with praise or wonder, are instances of the resistless force of perseverance: it is by this that the quarry becomes a pyramid, and the distant countries are united with canals. If a man was to compare the effect of a single stroke of the pick-ax, or of one impression of the spade with the general design and last result, he would be overwhelmed by the sense of their disproportion; yet those petty operations incessantly continued, in time surmount the greatest difficulties, and mountains are leveled, and oceans bounded, by the slender force of human beings.[1]

Prayer done in faith and perseverance is among those strokes that level the mountain.

Pray with Faith

In a "Hagar The Horrible" cartoon, a man in a tuxedo and top hat is shown pulling a wagon loaded with all sorts of trunks. The trunks are labeled with these captions: "Philosophies," "Ideas Big and Small," "Belief Systems," "Notions," "Theories," "Musings," and "Ologies." Hagar's son asks the man with the wagon, "What have you got that's *good?*"[2] That is an important question. The answer to such a question for us will be "faith."

In Luke 18:8, Jesus made a statement and asked a question that catch our attention: "I tell you, he will see that they get justice, and quickly. However, when the Son of Man comes, will he find faith on the earth?" If perseverance is important in prayer, then faith is even more important.

The widow in the parable kept approaching the judge because she believed that, sooner or later, he would give her what she needed. She had faith that something would happen. In telling the parable, Jesus implied that this same concept remains for people who pray. To pray with persistence and faith is to assure God's notice. This fact is not a "money-back guarantee" that everything will happen just as we want. I could not assure the young man who called me at 3:00 a.m. that the Lord would send him a wife by express mail. What I could do is to tell him that God cares about his dilemma and will work with him.

In November 1960, a six-year-old girl by the name of Ruby Bridges became the first black student in the formerly all-white William T. Frantz School in New Orleans. White parents lined up each day to shout slurs and curses at her as this child went to school accompanied by federal marshals. To everyone's amazement, little Ruby did not curse back. She prayed for the adults who lined the street leading to her school. Ruby had been told by her pastor that she should pray for people who persecute her and she took him at his word. Ruby's mother told a psychologist, "We're not asking her to pray for them because we want to hurt her or anything, but we think that we all have to pray for people like that, and we think Ruby should, too. Don't you think they need praying for?"[3]

Think of it. A six-year-old child taught a city how to pray in faith. The psychiatrist who interviewed Ruby finally concluded that he was mystified by her faith. He wrote, "The great paradox that Christ reminded us about is that sometimes those who are lonely and hurt and vulnerable—*meek*, to use the word—are touched by grace and can show the most extraordinary kind of dignity, and in that sense, inherit not only the next world, but even at times moments of this one. We who have so much knowledge and money and power look on confused, trying to mobilize the intellect, to figure things out. It is not so figurable, is it?"[4]

No, it really is not "figurable." The widow in the Bible and the kid in New Orleans trying to go to school displayed an attitude about life that should affect our prayers.

Pray with Humility

The parable of the Pharisee and the tax collector is one of the most familiar in the New Testament. Its very familiarity can cause us trouble, however. Note carefully to whom it was first preached. In verse 9 we learn that Jesus told the parable "to some who were confident of their own righteousness and looked down on everybody else."

The tax gatherers in Jesus' day were considered traitors because they helped the nation's enemies. The Pharisees, by contrast, were looked upon as men at the zenith of proper conduct and right attitude. They despised certain people, however, the chief among them being the tax gatherers.

Careful now. Part of the Pharisaic attitude in everyone is to look down on others. A person can be a snob about snobs, looking down on people who look down on people! Jesus' point in telling the story was to teach all believers that prayer is reaching out to God. Being in touch with the Creator of the universe is no trifling matter. Centuries ago, John Bunyan said, "Real prayer is a serious concern, for we are speaking to the Sovereign Lord of all the universe, who is willing to move heaven and earth in answer to sincere and reasonable prayer."[5]

Prayer that centers on our self-righteousness says, "Just look how great I am." This is the attitude that Jesus condemned. Why? Because our ego is not the point. I am not the center of the universe—God is. Any attitude that forgets that central fact is misguided.

The tax gatherer was justified before God because of his attitude. Confessing one's sins and pleading for God's forgiveness demonstrate praying with humility. That is what the tax gatherer did, and that is what Jesus commended.

Part of learning to pray is to humbly discover three categories that Fisher Humphreys describes.[6] First, there are some things God gives us whether we ask for them or not. He sends the sunshine and rain and oxygen to nourish our planet and us. We do not have to pray for those things. They are part of God's providence. Some things we get even if we do not ask.

Second, there are some things that we ask God for, but he will not grant our request. He is wiser than we are. Some requests do not fit into his long-range plans for humanity. Other things we ask for might be harmful to us. Some things we do not get even if we ask.

Third, there are some things that come our way only if we pray. This is the middle ground between the first and second categories. For his own purposes, God chooses to grant some things in life only if we ask for those things in prayer.

So what do we ask for? Our ignorance and immaturity often confuse us. We may not know what to ask for. Humphreys suggests that we are driven back to ask for what we think is in keeping with God's will for humankind:

> We ask, quite simply, for those things which we believe to be in keeping with God's purposes and thus to be best for ourselves and for those for whom we care: for food and peace for the world, for sensitivity to the needs of those around us, for a good education for our children, for strong and lasting friendships, for a vision of how we may serve God more productively, for healthy families, for guidance for those who must make decisions, for courage for the fearful, hope for the discouraged, wisdom for the confused, and health for the sick.[7]

We ask for what we believe is right. But we humbly admit that sometimes we do not know what is right. Even that can be a matter of prayer. The psalmist says in Psalm 5:3, "Morning by morning, O LORD, you hear my voice; / Morning by morning I lay my requests before you / and wait in expectation." We enter dialogue with God and then "wait in expectation" the way a lover waits for a return letter from her beloved.

Humility is needed in this because appearances and experience can be deceptive. Theologian Alister McGrath noted this well when he wrote the following:

> Experience cannot be allowed to have the final word—it must be judged and shown up as deceptive and misleading. A theology of the Cross draws our attention to the sheer unreliability of experience as a guide to the presence and activity of God. God is active and present in his world, quite independently of whether we experience him as being so. Experience declared that God was absent from Calvary, only to have its verdict humiliatingly overturned on the third day.[8]

Prayer allows for mystery to reside in the good intentions of God. The verdict of the Church is that, temporary appearances notwithstanding, God is worthy of our trust.

It's Your Turn Now

As we wrap up this chapter, think about your life right now. Give some thought to some of the challenges you face and face them with prayer. Consider these personal questions and comments:

- What are the two toughest problems you face right now?
- How can you begin to approach these problems with a healthy attitude?
- Can you, like the widow in the parable, persist in praying about these matters until things change? (Remember, the problems may not change, but your response to them might).
- Do you have any attitudes that need adjusting?

Perhaps you might want to start a prayer diary in which you chart your attitudes, your changes, and the ways God is working in your life.

Questions for Further Reflection

1. Have you ever felt like the young man who called at 3:00 a.m. and wanted an answer to prayer right now?
2. What does having perseverance in prayer really mean?
3. What does the parable about the unyielding widow and the unjust judge reveal about the character of God?
4. Reflect on the experience of the author's attempt to buy a house. Do problems like that have any significance as if God were trying to tell us something?
5. What does Ruby Bridges have to teach us about our attitudes and prayer?
6. For what in your life are you waiting "in expectation"?

5

Others Need Your Prayers

*"You have heard that it was said, 'Love your neighbor
and hate your enemy.' But I tell you: Love your enemies
and pray for those who persecute you, that you may be
sons of your Father in heaven. He causes his sun to rise
on the evil and the good, and sends rain on the righteous
and the unrighteous. If you love those who love you, what
reward will you get? Are not even the tax collectors doing
that? And if you greet only your brothers, what are you
doing more than others? Do not even pagans do that?
Be perfect, therefore, as your heavenly Father is
perfect."*

MATTHEW 5:43–48

*Jesus went through all the towns and villages, teaching in
their synagogues, preaching the good news of the kingdom
and healing every disease and sickness. When he saw the
crowds, he had compassion on them, because they were
harassed and helpless, like sheep without a shepherd.
Then he said to his disciples, "The harvest is plentiful but
the workers are few. Ask the Lord of the harvest, therefore,
to send out workers into his harvest field."*

MATTHEW 9:35–38

*"Simon, Simon, Satan has asked to sift you as wheat. But
I have prayed for you, Simon, that your faith may not fail.*

*And when you have turned back, strengthen your
brothers."*

*But he replied, "Lord, I am ready to go with you to
prison and to death."*

*Jesus answered, "I tell you, Peter, before the rooster
crows today, you will deny three times that you know me."*

LUKE 22:31–34

*When they came to the place called The Skull, there they
crucified him, along with the criminals—one on his right,
the other on his left. Jesus said, "Father, forgive them, for
they do not know what they are doing."*

LUKE 23:33–34

"I'll be praying for you." I hear this statement often in my
ministry, and I regularly tell this to people. Somehow just telling
people that you are calling their name before God helps them.
The late humorist, Lewis Grizzard, learned that fact late in his
life. He underwent serious heart surgery. Grizzard developed
complications that almost killed him. Speaking of those who cared
for him while he was in the hospital, he wrote, "To a man and
woman, those doctors and nurses said to me after the critical
time had passed, 'We exhausted all medical possibilities. We did
everything we knew to do for you, and it probably wouldn't
have been enough. What saved you was prayer.'"[1]

Grizzard had another serious problem with his heart that
finally took his life, but he went to his grave a changed man.
After the hospitalization mentioned above he wrote about all
the people who prayed for him:

> What I did to deserve any of that I don't know, but I do
> know I had spent a lot of time in my life doubting. At
> one time or the other, I doubted it all: spirituality, love,
> and the basic good of humankind. But this flirtation with
> the end of me has removed a lot of that doubt. If the
> medical experts say prayer brought me back from certain
> death, who am I to doubt them?[2]

Grizzard was onto something. He discovered for himself the
truth that praying for others *does* make a difference. Life matters.
God matters. Love matters.

Blaise Pascal, a seventeenth-century philosopher once wrote:

When I consider the short duration of my life, swallowed up in the eternity before and after, the little space which I fill and even can see, engulfed in the infinite immensity of spaces of which I am ignorant and which know me not, I am frightened and astonished at being here rather than there; for there is no reason why here rather than there, why now rather than then. Who has put me here? By whose order and direction have this place and time been allotted to me?[3]

Pascal was astonished that he had been given the gift of life at all. I am, too. What further astonishes me is that I have the ability to change my life and the lives of others by prayer. So do you.

Henry David Thoreau wrote:

However mean your life is, meet it and live it; do not shun it and call it hard names. It is not so bad, as you are. It looks poorest when you are richest. The fault-finder will find faults even in paradise. Love your life, poor as it is. Humility, like darkness, reveals the heavenly lights. Superfluous wealth can only buy superfluities. Money is not required to buy any necessary of the soul.[4]

Thoreau was onto something. Modest living helps us keep our eyes off ourselves and helps us to keep the focus on God. Being focused on something outside ourselves helps us see others as needy children, or potential children, of God. We can pray for them and lift them up.

We have been thinking about prayer through the pages of this book. We noticed that prayer is a central part of the Christian's walk with God. In this chapter we examine three different groups of people we should include in our prayers. Two groups are expected—Christian workers and our friends. The third group is unexpected—our enemies. Consider for a few minutes the concept of praying for people whose work is to serve Jesus Christ.

Pray for Christian Workers

One of the reasons why crowds flocked to Jesus, at least early in his ministry, is that the people could sense he cared about them. Jesus had compassion on the people because they seemed so helpless and directionless. He cared what happened to them. Contrast this with the attitude of the Pharisees. The Pharisees were concerned that Jesus was doing things that seemed to go against Jewish tradition. They were more concerned with their interpretation of the Law than they were with the well-being of the people. The Pharisees downgraded Jesus because he helped the man who was dumb. His action showed his compassion, whereas their action showed their lack of concern.

The people were like "sheep without a shepherd." Jesus said to his disciples that the people were like a great harvest ready to be reaped. All that was needed was a group of committed people gather it in.

Ask God to Send Workers

Jesus' instruction was, "Ask the Lord of the harvest, therefore, to send out workers into his harvest field." Jesus thus encouraged us to ask *earnestly* when we pray. You are to want something greatly and to keep asking until you receive it.

Jesus told his disciples to ask the Lord of the harvest—God himself—to send out workers into the ripe fields. God is willing to do his part. Let us do ours, also. We can pray for Christian workers who labor in various fields for the cause of Christ.

The needs of our world are enormous. The dilemma of people everywhere seems overwhelming at times. This fact only underscores the Christian's need to pray that God sends people to do some harvesting in his fields. We can do that by praying for Christian workers as they take the message of salvation to as many as possible.

Specific Ways to Pray

Here are some specific ways you can pray for Christian workers. First, begin with those closest to you. List the names of your pastor and other leaders in your own church, and then pray for them regularly. Next, think of some of the people in your area and your state who need your prayers.

Do you know some of the leaders of your denomination or other ministries? Pray next for missionaries, both at home and in foreign places. Now pray for yourself, that you may be one of the workers Christ will use.

Remember that praying is work. It is real, effort-filled toil. You struggle to pray and to keep praying even when you do not see instant results. Charles Rabon was correct when he wrote, "God has no microwave saints. They aren't made that easily or quickly."[5] Our prayers affect others, but they change us, too.

Pray for Your Friends

How would you like Jesus himself to pray for you? I can hardly imagine a more impressive spiritual gesture. In Luke's gospel, Jesus told Simon Peter that he had prayed for him. The setting was a dispute among Jesus' disciples about who was the greatest. They had not yet learned that in God's eyes, greatness is not a matter of personal pride. Greatness is measured in service to others. Thus, Jesus explained, "[T]he greatest among you should become like the youngest, and the one who rules like the one who serves"(Lk. 22:26). Jesus said to Peter, "Simon, Simon, Satan has asked to sift you as wheat. But I have prayed for you, Simon, that your faith may not fail. And when you have turned back, strengthen your brothers"(Lk. 22:31–32).

This prayer was for Jesus' friend and disciple, Simon Peter. We may follow Jesus' example when we pray for our friends' success in overcoming temptation. As a pastor I personally know when other people are praying for me. I also pray for others whom I know are facing various trials and temptations. Our mutual prayers benefit each other.

Jesus' prayer for Simon helped not only him, but others as well. Had Peter failed and turned his back on Christ, many people would not have known of God's love through Peter's later witness. We may never know what wider benefits accrue when we pray for our friends and acquaintances.

Many people have prayer lists, written or mental, filled with people for whom they pray regularly. Some have been lifting the names of friends and family for many years, sometimes without any visible results. But they keep at it because they realize that visible results are often misleading.

Frank Wright tells the story of Emilio Franco, who lost his voice due to a nervous disorder during World War II. In 1949, Mr. Franco took his family on a vacation to Coney Island. While there Franco rode the Cyclone, one of the largest and most terrifying roller coasters at that time. On one of the Cyclone's steep descents Franco regained his voice—he began screaming! When the ride ended and he got off, Emilio Franco spoke his first words since the war—"I feel sick."[6]

Sometimes our words come hard. They are almost pried out of us one at a time. At other times they are literally scared from our throats. Sometimes even prayer seems like that. If you find yourself having a difficult time praying for others, even your family and friends, be patient with yourself. Ask God to help you pray. Sometimes words failed even the apostle Paul. He once wrote:

> In the same way, the Spirit helps us in our weakness. We do not know what we ought to pray for, but the Spirit himself intercedes for us with groans that words cannot express. And he who searches our hearts knows the mind of the Spirit, because the Spirit intercedes for the saints in accordance with God's will. (Rom. 8:26–27)

Pray for Your Enemies: What Jesus Taught

Anyone, whether Christian or not, can understand the concept of wanting the best for one's friends. Many non-Christian people genuinely love their friends and families. These people would have no trouble with Jesus' teaching about praying for friends. What would make them gasp in amazement is the remainder of his teaching. Jesus did not stop at telling us to pray for our friends. We are also to pray for our enemies!

In Matthew 5—7, we hear from Jesus in his Sermon on the Mount. He laid out a blueprint for the kingdom of God. Part of that design is that people who call his name should extend their concern beyond their own families and friends. They should reach out even to people who they do not like.

Jesus said, "Love your enemies, and pray for those who persecute you." Love your enemies! What a command that is. We might feel more like cursing them or ignoring them. Praying for them is probably the last thing on our minds. But the attitude of the Christian is no longer his or her own. As Paul put it in Philippians 2:5, "Your attitude should be the same as that of Christ Jesus."

Praying for his or her enemies distinguishes the Christian from everyone else. It is appropriate behavior for followers of Jesus. One person who took this call seriously was a man named Magnus Sacatus Patricius, better known to most as Saint Patrick. He took the gospel to Ireland in the fifth century. Patrick's father was a deacon in the church in Britain, and his influence affected his son. When Patrick was 16 years old, pirates from Ireland attacked the villa he lived in. The boy and many others were enslaved and carried back to Ireland.

He was sold as a slave to a tribal chieftain who put him to work herding pigs. Patrick remembered his father's teaching about Christ and was converted in this foreign land. He came to be known as "Holy Boy" because of his devotion to God. After six years of slavery, Patrick escaped and made his way home.

After being at home for a while, Patrick surprised his family by telling them that he was going to return to Ireland as Christ's messenger. He wrote in his book, *Confessions,* "I did not go back to Ireland of my own accord. It is not in my own nature to show mercy toward the very ones who once enslaved me."[7] Concerning his work as a missionary, he wrote, "It was the furthest thing from me, but God made me fit, causing me to care about and labor for the salvation of others."[8]

By the end of his thirty-year ministry in Ireland, Patrick had seen 100,000 converts and the establishment of many churches. He was one who took seriously Christ's words, "Pray for those who persecute you."

Think about some of the impersonal forces that you consider as enemies, such as poverty, disease, and so on, which you intend to pray about. Now put some faces on you enemies and jot down the names of people you consider enemies (or at least non-friends). Make a point to pray for them this week.

Pray for Your Enemies: What Jesus Did

I sometimes hear people say things like, "Jesus was a good teacher, but nothing more." They seem to assume that Jesus' teaching and actions did not mesh perfectly. His teaching was that people should pray for their enemies. Saying this while comfortable and safe, as on the mountainside surrounded by disciples, is one thing. Practicing it under horrible conditions is quite another.

During the final day of his earthly life, Jesus was crucified on a cross. This was a tortuous death. If he had gone back on his teaching, surely it would have been at that time. But look at what happened. Luke 23:34 reports, "Jesus said, 'Father, forgive them, for they do not know what they are doing.'" He not only taught that one should pray for his enemies, he also set the example himself.

I heard of a letter that was found in a baking powder can wired to the handle of an old pump. The pump offered the only drinking water on a long and seldom-used trail across the Amargosa Desert. The letter read:

> "This pump is all right as of June 1932. I put a new sucker washer into it and it ought to last five years. But the washer dries out and the pump has got to be primed. Under the white rock I buried a bottle of water, out of the sun and cork end up. There's enough water to prime the pump, but not if you drink some first. Pour about one fourth and let her soak the leather. Then pour in the rest medium fast and pump like crazy. You'll git water. The well has never run dry. Have faith. When you git watered up, fill the bottle and put it back like you found it for the next feller. [Signed] Desert Pete."[9]

Praying for an enemy is a lot like that. It is an act of faith that "primes the pump" in relationships. It also gives something back for the coming generation because it helps break the cycle of hate and fear. It's *tough!* But it's necessary.

It's Your Turn Now

This chapter is entitled "Others Need Your Prayers." That is a statement of fact. We have considered several ways you could put into effect the central truth of this fact. Here are several other suggestions for you that might help you better pray for others.

- For starters, you might thank God for the times when others have prayed for you.
- You could make a prayer list on which you put the names of people and situations that you know could use your prayers.
- Keep it up-to-date as you add some to it and take others off. Read other books on prayer.
- Attend prayer meetings with other people.
- More important than all this, however, you could pray that God would use *you* as a Christian worker. Be careful what you pray for, though. You might get it.

Questions for Further Reflection

1. What does it mean to ask God to send workers? Who are they? Are you among that number?
2. Imagine that Jesus is praying for you. What difference do you think that would make?
3. Is praying for your enemies realistic today? Was it ever realistic?
4. Can you think of one or two people who might be classified as your enemies? Will you pray for (not against) them once a day for a week and see what happens?
5. Reflect on Paul's confession in Romans 8:26–27. Does that sometimes describe your experience with prayer?

6

Honesty in Prayer

*Because the LORD revealed their plot to me, I knew it, for
at that time he showed me what they were doing. I had
been like a gentle lamb led to the slaughter; I did not
realize that they had plotted against me, saying,*

> *"Let us destroy the tree and its fruit;*
> *let us cut him off from the land of the living,*
> *that his name be remembered no more."*
> *But, O LORD Almighty, you who judge righteously*
> *and test the heart and mind,*
> *let me see your vengeance upon them,*
> *for to you I have committed my cause.*

*"Therefore this is what the LORD says about the men of
Anathoth who are seeking your life and saying, 'Do not
prophesy in the name of the LORD or you will die by our
hands'—therefore this is what the LORD Almighty says: 'I
will punish them. Their young men will die by the sword,
their sons and daughters by famine. Not even a remnant
will be left to them, because I will bring disaster on the
men of Anathoth in the year of their punishment.'"*

> *You are always righteous, O LORD, when I bring a case*
> *before you.*
> *Yet I would speak with you about your justice:*

Why does the way of the wicked prosper?
Why do all the faithless live at ease?
You have planted them, and they have taken root;
      they grow and bear fruit.
You are always on their lips
      but far from their hearts.
Yet you know me, O Lord;
      you see me and test my thoughts about you.
Drag them off like sheep to be butchered!
      Set them apart for the day of slaughter!
How long will the land lie parched
      and the grass in every field be withered?
Because those who live in it are wicked,
      the animals and birds have perished.
Moreover, the people are saying,
      "He will not see what happens to us."

"If you have raced with men on foot
      and they have worn you out,
      how can you compete with horses?
If you stumble in safe country,
      how will you manage in the thickets by the Jordan?
Your brothers, your own family—
      even they have betrayed you;
      they have raised a loud cry against you.
Do not trust them,
      though they speak well of you.

Jeremiah 11:18–12:6

"O Lord, you deceived me, and I was deceived;
      you overpowered me and prevailed.
I am ridiculed all day long;
      everyone mocks me.
Whenever I speak, I cry out
      proclaiming violence and destruction.
So the word of the Lord has brought me
      insult and reproach all day long.
But if I say, "I will not mention him
      or speak any more in his name,"
his word is in my heart like a burning fire,

shut up in my bones.
I am weary of holding it in;
indeed, I cannot.
I hear many whispering,
"Terror on every side!
Report him! Let's report him!"
All my friends
are waiting for me to slip, saying,
"Perhaps he will be deceived;
then we will prevail over him
and take our revenge on him."

But the LORD *is with me like a mighty warrior;*
so my persecutors will stumble and not prevail.
They will fail and be thoroughly disgraced;
their dishonor will never be forgotten.
O LORD *Almighty, you who examine the righteous*
and probe the heart and mind,
let me see your vengeance upon them,
for to you I have committed my cause.
Sing to the LORD!
Give praise to the LORD!
He rescues the life of the needy
from the hands of the wicked.
Cursed be the day I was born!
May the day my mother bore me not be blessed!
Cursed be the man who brought my father the news,
who made him very glad, saying,
"A child is born to you—a son!"
May that man be like the towns
the LORD *overthrew without pity.*
May he hear wailing in the morning,
a battle cry at noon.
For he did not kill me in the womb,
with my mother as my grave,
her womb enlarged forever.
Why did I ever come out of the womb
to see trouble and sorrow
and to end my days in shame?

JEREMIAH 20:7–18

"If God knew how I really felt, I'm not sure what he would do." Thus began a conversation with a friend on the nature of God and the friend's doubts. We were not long into the conversation before I discovered that this friend felt like he was the only person having difficulty with faith. To his relief I showed him that others, even in the Bible, have had trouble with their religious commitments. Jeremiah was one such person. For him faith was not an escape from reality. It was just the opposite—a movement toward the source of all truth and reality. That source is God.

In this chapter, which is longer than previous chapters, we will look at the matter of honesty toward God in prayer. We will examine what the prophet Jeremiah had to say about his encounters with God and his fellow countrymen. From this we will discover many truths about prayer, but one will especially stand out—prayer is radical honesty.

My friend's comment mentioned above is important. First, he thought that God did not know how he felt—"If God knew…" Second, he thought that even if God did know, the Lord would be angry or disappointed. Third, he felt that the road to faith and piety lay in hiding feelings and doubts rather than exposing them to the fresh air of Scripture, shared wisdom, and honest prayer. In short, my friend, and probably countless others, wondered about this fundamental question of faith: "Can I be completely honest with God, and tell him my doubts and complaints as well as my faith and strength?"

An excellent way to get at that question is by examining the life and teaching of the prophet Jeremiah, a man of deep feeling. He grieved over the status of his country and its plunge into disaster. He was no "armchair quarterback," but was in the game at all times. This strong and sensitive man was honest with himself about his feelings. He made no attempt to hid or bury them. This openness led him also to be honest with God. We see Jeremiah's struggle with his doubts, compounded by his feelings that God was unfair.

Piety or Blasphemy?

To some contemporary Christians fed on the cotton candy fluff of some modern teaching, Jeremiah's words sound like blasphemy. His comment is not a "name it and claim it" boost. It has no "victory" sound to it. Did the prophet stand with white marks on his sandals as he inched up to the chalk mark separating honesty from blasphemy? Part of the answer can be found by examining the opening of chapter 12.

Jeremiah began his prayer, not with rage or impertinence, but with a reverent salutation: "You are always righteous, O LORD…" Only after such a greeting could he then lay out his feelings before God. The mood reminds us of Jesus in the garden of Gethsemane on the night of his arrest. He prayed, "Father, if you are willing, take this cup from me; yet not my will, but yours be done" (Lk. 22:42).

Jeremiah did not accuse God of injustice. He did not bring a case *against* God, but rather *before* him. This prophet pleads his case with God. What was the problem? He was troubled about the matter of justice, or in this case, what seemed like injustice: "Why does the way of the wicked prosper?" Jeremiah looked around him and saw his nation falling apart. Trouble seemed to be brewing on every side. The godly, seeming to be in small numbers, were not faring well. The ungodly, in vast numbers, seemed to prosper. Jeremiah could not understand it. He wondered if God was diligent about the matters of earth. This notion is expressed in other places in the Bible, most notably in the Psalms.

Psalm 73:1–14 is a good example. The first five verses read,

Surely God is good to Israel,
to those who are pure in heart!
But as for me, my feet had almost slipped;
I had nearly lost my foothold.
For I envied the arrogant
when I saw the prosperity of the wicked.
They have no struggles;
their bodies are healthy and strong.
They are free from the burdens common to man;
they are not plagued by human ills.

This situation seemed to be a reversal of the rules. The righteous were supposed to prosper and the wicked were supposed to vanish, weren't they?

It did not work out that way for Jeremiah, and it often does not today. Sometimes the roles seem reversed, almost to the point of appearing that that is the way it is supposed to be! I have a friend who worked on an oil-drilling rig in Louisiana. He felt a call to become a minister and accepted it. On the last day on the rig before going back to school, a piece of steel fell out of the derrick and struck my friend on the side of the head. He suffered a severe brain injury and lives with constant pain. He is damaged for life and has no chance to fulfill his call. Why do the righteous suffer?

On the other hand, I heard of two brothers who owned a men's store in New York. Someone would come in to look at suits and one brother would wait on him. If the customer asked, "How much is this suit?" the man waiting on him would say, "I don't know. Let me find out." Then he would yell across the store, "Hey Mort, how much is this gray pinstripe?" His brother would yell back, "One ninety-nine ninety-five." Then the first brother working with the customer would pretend to be hard of hearing and say to the customer, "Mort says it's one thirty-nine ninety-five." The customer, who just heard the price quoted at $199.95, thought he was getting a steal and would buy the suit immediately. Why do those who do not play straight prosper? Only God knows.

Jeremiah's preaching was not well received by his country-men. The people of false piety in his hometown of Anathoth (12:2) and even his own family (12:6) did not want the prophet's message. They had even plotted against his life (11:19). All of this came after he tried to serve God faithfully, but seemed to get nowhere. Thus, his complaint in 12:1 came pouring out.

People of genuine faith may address their doubts and questions to God in prayer. This is what Jeremiah did, and what we today may do. It is not blasphemy to raise genuine questions and doubts to God. It is instead a sign of deep trust.

God's Answer

When Jeremiah spoke openly to God, the Lord returned the favor. He spoke freely to the prophet. The answer God provided in Jeremiah 12:5 is something for which Jeremiah was not searching. Perhaps he expected the Lord to say something like this, "Yes, Jeremiah, you are right. I've been negligent, but I promise to do better. From now on, you can rest assured that I will be watching out for you a little better." After all, had not Jeremiah committed his life and work to God? (See 11:20.)

God's answer to Jeremiah is more a challenge than an easy answer. He challenged the prophet to grow, to get stronger, to prepare himself for the future battles that would be much tougher than the ones already fought. James Leo Green has paraphrased God's answer in verse 5 this way:

> "If a few foot runners have worn you out in your race for me, what will you do when you come up against thoroughbred horses? And if you fall flat on you face on level ground in a pleasant meadowland as you move for me, what will you do in the tangled, lion-infested jungles of the Jordan? The days are coming which will make these days look like easy days. There are higher hurdles ahead. You are up against boys now. There are men farther down the road, and farther still, giants. Cheer up, Jeremiah, the worst is yet to come!"[1]

What comfort!

One who reads the Bible seriously learns quickly that God seldom gives simple, trite answers to our questions. Instead, God challenges us to grow and develop spiritually. He wanted Jeremiah to get stronger in his smaller trials so that when the larger ones came, he would be ready. Genuine prayer, as I have indicated before, is no trivial pursuit.

Think back over the last two years of your life. Have you encountered anything you might consider as "light" trials that might prepare you for things to come? Perhaps you felt overwhelmed already and hoped nothing worse would come along. Why not make this a matter of prayer? Speak openly to God about it. But remember, you may get an unexpected answer.

Accusing God!

You have to hand it to Jeremiah. Whatever else he might have been, he was not a coward. After his initial complaint in

12:1, he moved on in his relationship to God. As that relationship grew and developed, so did the prophet's boldness. In 20:7 we see Jeremiah accusing God of deceit:

> O LORD, you deceived me and I was deceived;
> you overpowered me and prevailed.
> I am ridiculed all day long;
> everyone mocks me.

This accusation, which runs from verse 7 through verse 18, has been called "one of the most powerful and impressive passages in the whole of the prophetic literature, a passage which takes us, as no other, not only into the depths of the prophet's soul, but into the secrets of the prophetic consciousness."[2]

Although Jeremiah felt deceived, he at least felt there was a divine purpose in all of this—that is, that God was doing this for some purpose. Even so, this passage illustrates the suffering involved in living one's life in faithfulness to God. The word "deceived" in verse 7 is used in Exodus 22:16 for the rape of a virgin, and in Judges 16:5 of Delilah's seduction of Samson. Jeremiah felt that God had seduced, enticed, and tricked him into surrendering his life. That caused Jeremiah great anguish later on. We can imagine why. If God is not trustworthy, who is?

Jeremiah felt a deep personal hurt. Not only did he feel abandoned by friends and family, but he also felt tricked by God. When a person feels this low, there is nowhere else to go but up. But the climb back up was not accomplished in an instant, or even in a day. For Jeremiah to come to terms with his circumstances took a lifetime. He poured out his anger and sense of outrage to God all the while.

Do you begin to see how all of this relates to prayer? Earlier I called prayer radical honesty. Jeremiah certainly felt honest toward God, honest enough to wonder if God was having a belly laugh at his expense. Was the whole business a kind of celestial joke? What was going on? Jeremiah, like many before and after him, began to realize that prayer is no child's game. C. S. Lewis once said, "Prayer is either a sheer illusion or a personal contact between embryonic, incomplete persons (ourselves) and the utterly concrete Person."[3]

Rejection and Betrayal

To feel tricked by God is bad enough, but to feel cut off from friends and family compounds the wound. Jeremiah had known that some of his family had rejected him (12:6), and some had even plotted to kill him (11:19). He stood up under this pressure for a while, but it began to get to him. In 20:8 and 10 he expressed his great hurt to God. Jeremiah said in verse 8 that he had faithfully done his duty, as he understood it. In the previous verse he noted that he had become a laughingstock for the people. No one likes to be ridiculed! It is a painful thing to be laughed at, but to be scorned when you think you are doing God's will is even harder to take! Yet this was Jeremiah's trouble.

He said that each time he spoke, he proclaimed violence and destruction. But what did his faithfulness to his Lord get him? Laughter and ridicule. The people did not want a word of judgment and woe. They wanted someone to tell them they would be victorious. Jeremiah's preaching had little effect other than to antagonize the people.

In verse 10 he related to the Lord that the people had made a joke of his preaching. Can't you just hear them, as they would say something like this? "Hey look, there's old 'Terror-on-every-side.' Come on. Let's have some fun. Hey, 'Terror,' what news do you have for us today? Are we going to fall today?" This would be followed by peals of laughter from the people. Ridiculing is always easier than working. Sneering is less costly than being faithful. The majority of the people thought of Jeremiah as little more than an anachronism, a stage joke to be scorned. He said,

> All my friends
> are waiting for me to slip, saying,
> "Perhaps he will be deceived;
>> then we will prevail over him
>> and take our revenge on him." (v. 10b)

Thus Jeremiah knew scorn, the abandonment of friends and family, and plots against himself.

How did he stand up under such pressure? The last part of verse 12 gives us the clue: "for to you I have committed my cause." Check out his reasons.

- He believed that God was with him (v. 11).
- He felt that his enemies would not prevail because he was on God's side.
- He thought that the Lord saw the heart and the mind of both he and his detractors.

His position was neither easy nor enviable, but he did not give up. He was, however, tempted to quit.

Tempted to Quit

A friend of mine left the professional ministry several years ago. Many relationships in his life soured. Neither work nor home was much source of comfort or joy. He resigned his position, divorced his wife, and moved to another state and began working for a secular organization. This man's name could be "Legion," for he is many. Each year hundreds of preachers resign their positions and enter secular work. They get burned out and used up. While the term "burnout" seems to be new, the condition it describes is as old as Jeremiah.

In verse 9 of chapter 20 of Jeremiah, the prophet expressed his desire to stop preaching. What good had it done? All he could see was the pain it caused him. We should remember that this verse is set in the larger context of a prayer, which begins at verse 7 and goes through verse 18. Jeremiah was saying this to God. This is well in keeping with his honesty and openness to his Lord. He said,

> But if I say, "I will not mention him
>   or speak any more in his name,"
>   his word is in my heart like a burning fire,
>   shut up in my bones.
> I am weary of holding it in; indeed,
>   I cannot.

Jeremiah was telling the One who had called and commissioned him that he had had enough. The experience was too painful. The prophet found, however, that he could not turn off the inner conviction of his heart the way we today turn off a light switch. Whenever he tried to stop thinking about God or speaking in God's name, Jeremiah found that he could not control his mind. He could not forget.

Like a fire burning inside him, a fire that could not be contained, the word of God kept demanding expression. Jeremiah found that he was not in control any longer. This does not mean that he was a mere robot or puppet controlled by God. Instead, the message from his Lord had become so much a part of Jeremiah that he could not cut it off without injuring himself. His sense of calling was real, and his relationship with God was so deep and personal that it was too intertwined in his life to forget it.

I am married and have twin sons. Most of the time I am very happy in my home life, but sometimes I get angry or disappointed. Suppose I said one day, "Well, if that's the way you're going to treat me, I'll just leave." I pack my suitcase and leave. What would happen the next day? This has never happened in my home, but I feel sure I would go right back. Why? My relationship with my wife and children are too much a vital part of my life simply to forget or turn off.

This simple illustration is, I think, something that will offer a clue to verse 9. Jeremiah wanted to do what was right. He had a deep and abiding faith in God, and he spoke what he believed to be God's message to his fellow countrymen. All he got for his trouble was ridicule. He thought about abandoning his prophetic vocation, but found he had been with it too long. It had become a living part of him and not just something he did out of expectation or coercion.

The Word lived in him and it bubbled to the surface and demanded expression. However we think about this, what is important is to realize is that Jeremiah was saying two important things at the same time. First, he was stating his fatigue and stress, thus his comment about wanting to stop speaking in God's name. Second, he was indicating that his relationship with God was too deep to lay aside. He felt too strongly about his prophetic vocation simply to abandon it. His words sound like those of Paul in 1 Corinthians 9:16: "Woe to me if I do not preach the gospel." This is both divine compulsion and personal expression.

Christians today face this same dilemma as Jeremiah. We sometimes feel tired and at the end of our ropes. We get weary of trying to be lighthouses in a dark world, of turning the other cheek while others take advantage of us, of always giving while others seem only to get. When we reach this state, remembering Jeremiah in verse 9 will help us. As God rekindled Jeremiah's sense of call, so the Lord can renew our sense of call and commission.

Does this lesson apply to you personally? To someone you know well? Consider ways you might open yourself to God's renewing of your relationship to him. Keeping a relationship open to God in prayer is not always easy. As you grow in your faith you will experience times that seem silent. But don't give up. Remember what we called prayer in an earlier chapter—a fierce conversation. Like Jeremiah, you can renew your faith.

Renewed Faith

After all the complaining, after all the expression of deceit, after all the feelings of dread, Jeremiah came finally to realize that his situation was not hopeless. He felt himself answerable to God, and at the same time, felt that God was answerable to him. This was not arrogance on Jeremiah's part. It was an expression of his faith that God would not leave him alone and defenseless. God would answer him and come to him. Verse 11 is the prophet's confession of faith. God was with him and his enemies would not prevail against him.

Jeremiah called the Lord a "mighty warrior." Jeremiah expressed his belief that, despite all the setbacks and the ups and downs of his faith, he still believed that God would be his champion or warrior. God would assure the victory of his faith.

This description of God as a warrior sounds strange to the ears of contemporary Christians. We are nursed on the milk of peace and harmony. We are nurtured on the solid food of Jesus' words about turning the other cheek. What could Jeremiah's description of God in such a military fashion mean? The words of one commentator might be helpful here:

> [I]t is a description of God's person essential to the biblical witness. Jeremiah's God is at war against Judah's sin, just

as surely as he is also at war against ours. Jeremiah has heard the sounds and seen the sights of that coming war...and they are dreadful in their portent. Jeremiah knows, according to the words of this confession, that God's judgment on Judah will come and that therefore his preaching of doom will be vindicated, while those who scorn his message will be eternally dishonored, as they are at this day. God is not Lord unless he wars against human defiance of him, and he is not good except he be also an enemy of our evil. So over against all our attempts to have it our own way, over against every desire of ours to compromise his will, stands this dread Warrior God of this prophet of Judah."[4]

God was thus the "champion" for Jeremiah in that the Lord is at war with sin. The prophet's confidence in God's saving presence was the thing that raised him up out of his sense of despair. As shown above, Jeremiah felt that he had been deceived about what God was doing and required of him. When he saw the wicked prosper he wondered if God had not made some mistake! Finally, however, Jeremiah thought seriously about the nature of God. He realized that whatever appearances might indicate, God was still in charge. The history of Judah was unfolding to indicate that God was indeed at war with rebellion and sin. What Jeremiah was trying to get his people to see was that they were digging their own graves.

In all of this, Jeremiah was open in his relationship with God. He was so open that his honesty is transparent. The ancient prophet has much to teach contemporary Christians in this regard. For Jeremiah, the opposite of reverence is not honesty, but apathy. We need not be overly concerned about "offending" God with our honesty. I am not suggesting that we treat God disrespectfully! My point is that deep belief creates strong convictions and feelings. These convictions and feelings are sometimes contradicted and opposed by certain events in our world. We sometimes hear well-meaning people say, "Just pray and everything will be all right." But not everything is all right. Loved ones die. We have financial struggles and setbacks. Personal relationships get fouled up.

The trouble with this simplistic thinking is that it is not biblical. Jeremiah knew that no amount of false piety would ever bring him to a deeper understanding of God's purposes in this world. Read the first eight chapters of Job and Paul's letter to the Philippians. You will discover two men wrestling with things that have gone wrong, things not according to their plans. But you will also discover two men who were honest with God and who would not give up. Such was the case with Jeremiah. Like Jacob wrestling with the angel at Jabbok (Gen. 32:24–32), Jeremiah refused to give up until he was blessed.

That is our clue. In all openness and honesty refuse to give up. Allow God to be God and keep the relationship alive by your fierce conversations with him. This is not always easy, but it is always worth the effort.

It's Your Turn Now

We can learn to pray by thinking of our prayers as our speaking to an intimate friend. True friendship rests on honesty. A deep faith relationship does, too. This does not insult God or make him any less God. It draws us closer to him and lets us know that he understands and cares. God cares. He really cares. This is the best thing we might learn from Jeremiah.

Here are some other realities that we learned in this chapter:

- Honesty can be reverent and reverence can be honest.
- God is tough enough to hear any question you have, or to shoulder any feeling you bring to him.
- Our pilgrimage of faith and prayer is not a smooth road. It is often a rocky, rut-filled path through the wilderness.
- You grow the most when, like Jeremiah, you find your ideas challenged and have to keep relearning about God.
- In order to put into practice what you have learned, you might want to begin keeping a prayer journal. This is some sort of notebook in which you record your prayers and answers to your prayers. It would include honest questions and deep feelings, such as Jeremiah had. You might just find your prayer life revolutionized.

Questions for Further Reflection

1. Are you shocked and disturbed or comforted by Jeremiah's honesty with God?
2. Have there been times when you felt betrayed by everyone, including God?
3. This chapter began with this sentence: "If God knew how I really felt, I'm not sure what he could do." How do you react to such a statement?

(continued)

4. God's answers to Jeremiah's complaints do not seem very soft or comforting. What do you think God was trying to teach Jeremiah?

5. Have there been times when you, like Jeremiah, have been tempted to quit serving God or trying to learn more about him?

6. Jeremiah called God a "mighty warrior." What does that mean?

7. If you were to be absolutely honest with God at this moment—to have a "fierce conversation"—what would you say to him?

7

God Will Strengthen You through Prayer

Then Jesus went with his disciples to a place called Gethsemane, and he said to them, "Sit here while I go over there and pray." He took Peter and the two sons of Zebedee along with him, and he began to be sorrowful and troubled. Then he said to them, "My soul is overwhelmed with sorrow to the point of death. Stay here and keep watch with me."

Going a little farther, he fell with his face to the ground and prayed, "My Father, if it is possible, may this cup be taken from me. Yet not as I will, but as you will."

Then he returned to his disciples and found them sleeping. "Could you men not keep watch with me for one hour?" he asked Peter. "Watch and pray so that you will not fall into temptation. The spirit is willing, but the body is weak."

He went away a second time and prayed, "My Father, if it is not possible for this cup to be taken away unless I drink it, may your will be done."

When he came back, he again found them sleeping, because their eyes were heavy. So he left them and went away once more and prayed the third time, saying the same thing.

*Then he returned to the disciples and said to them,
"Are you still sleeping and resting? Look, the hour is near,
and the Son of Man is betrayed into the hands of sinners.
Rise, let us go! Here comes my betrayer!"*

MATTHEW 26:36–46

"Oh, good…you're not busy." That is the tag line on a cartoon
that shows a pastor in his study. He is kneeling in prayer as the
secretary comes in with a handful of papers. She looks down,
sees the pastor praying, and says, "Oh, good…you're not busy."

What do you make of this situation? Is he busy with
something momentous and urgent, or is he just fiddling with
some trifle until he has something better to do? I can answer
that question from my own experience as a minister. Without
prayer, I'm as good as dead.

We human beings are weak and needy creatures. That is
because we are so complex and full of potential. Our very
potential marks us for temptation and weakness. Temptations
are downward pulls that touch us at important points in our
lives. We are seldom tempted with something unimportant. For
instance, sexual temptations are strong and persistent. People
are vulnerable to this problem because the Lord himself made
us sexual beings and said to Adam and Eve, "Be fruitful and
multiply." This may be the only divine command that humanity
has taken up with gusto! The point here is that this is a major
and vital aspect of our lives. We are susceptible to falling just
because sex is so important.

In all times of testing, temptation, and grief, we can seek
spiritual strength through prayer. Throughout the previous
chapters on prayer we have seen that prayer is not magic or a
gimmick that allows us to get whatever we desire. Prayer is our
hearts communicating with the heart of God. It is our minds
pouring themselves out to the mind of God. Prayer is essentially
personal in that it takes all that we are and gives it to God. Jesus
shows us how to pray when we need God's strength.

Pray to Do God's Will

If you knew you were about to die, what would you do?
This was not an academic question for Jesus as he took his

disciples to Gethsemane. He knew that something was about to break. He had come to die for mankind and was preparing to see the end of his life.

Jesus took his disciples to the garden. He stationed most of them at a key position and took Peter, James, and John to a more central location. The scripture says Jesus "began to be sorrowful and troubled. Then he said to them, 'My soul is overwhelmed with sorrow to the point of death. Stay here and keep watch with me'" (vv. 37b–38). Here was Jesus himself, the very Son of God, in grief and anguish. How did he deal with his dilemma? He prayed.

Prayer is sometimes a wrestling match of the soul, a wrestling match with God. Jesus told a parable about an unjust judge to teach that people should keep praying and searching and not to give up (Lk. 18:1–8). This perseverance is often called importunity. Curtis Mitchell has written, "Importunity is an instructor in God's school of Christian development. In short, God does not become more willing to answer because of perseverance, but the petitioner may become more capable of receiving the answer."[1]

I think British theologian P. T. Forsyth was on target when he wrote:

> Lose the importunity of prayer, reduce it to soliloquy, or even colloquy, with God, lose the real conflict of will and will, lose the habit of wrestling and the hope of prevailing with God, make it mere walking with God in friendly talk; and precious as it is, yet you tend to lose the reality of prayer at last.[2]

Life's most important decisions require life's most important resources. One of those is prayer.

Jesus *could* have done other things. He could have called in the legions of angels to help him. He could have given up on mankind and let them all be damned. But with the entire arsenal of heaven at his disposal, Jesus chose prayer as the one right weapon with which to fight this battle. It was right because prayer helps to establish and maintain a relationship with God. Prayer helps us do the things of God in God's way. God's way is to love human beings. Jesus prayed so he could love us enough to do whatever it took, even being crucified of a cross.

If it was right for Jesus, then it is equally right for us. Praying for spiritual strength is appropriate in times of grief and distress. When death comes to loved ones, pray. When temptations come, pray. When plans are shattered, pray. Prayer is personal communication between you and God. It can never be out of place.

Matthew tells us that Jesus went a bit further away from his three closest friends and prayed more. The content of that prayer shows the difference between prayer that is self-centered and prayer that is God-centered. Jesus said, "My Father, if it is possible, may this cup be taken from me. Yet not as I will, but as you will." The "cup" spoken of here was the total experience of anguish Jesus felt and his death on a cross shortly to take place.

Jesus did not want to die. Like any man, he wanted to live as long as possible. Thus he prayed, "if it is possible, may this cup be taken from me." In another sense, though, he realized that life was more than protecting himself. Thus, he continued, "Yet not as I will, but as you will." The word *yet* made all the difference in the world. He wanted relief and deliverance, but he was willing to accept whatever came because he trusted God. Jesus felt the great anguish of the occasion and, in a way, wanted out of it. Even so, he could say to God, "Yet I do not choose my way, but I choose *your* way."

Praying to *know* God's will is one thing. Praying to *do* it is something else. We explore this matter further in the next chapter. Here let us simply realize that knowing the will of God is only the first step on a process. Doing that will requires faith and courage. We Christians should pray to find God's strength in times of stress. But we should also commit ourselves to do God's will regardless of the outcome.

I once tried to talk to a certain man about God. He told me that when he was young his grandmother with whom he lived became ill. He prayed that she would get well, but she died instead. He said, "If God is real and hears prayer, why didn't he answer me?" Anyone can pray, but not everyone is prepared to accept God's answer. That man did not seem to realize that God had said "no" to his prayer. Jesus' prayer in Gethsemane indicates that he knew the difference between calling on God to get our way and calling on God to find *his* way. We may legitimately call upon the Lord for anything that concerns us. We should seek what God wants for us so we can do his will. This is not always easy, but it is always important.

Sometimes the temptation is to give in to despair and quit serving God. This happens especially when we are overcome with grief. Author Richard Exley tells about a pastor whose son committed suicide. Even in this situation the pastor overcame the temptation to be overcome by sorrow. He returned to the pulpit ten days later and read from Roman 8:28: "And we know that in all things God works for the good of those who love him, who have been called according to his purpose." Then he told his congregation where he was with all that had happened:

> I cannot make my son's suicide fit into this passage. It's impossible for me to see how anything good can come out of it. I realize that I only see in part. I only know in part. It's like the miracle of the shipyard. Almost every part of our great oceangoing vessels are made of steel. If you take any single part—be it a steel plate out of the hull or the huge rudder—and throw it into the ocean, it will sink. Steel doesn't float! But when shipbuilders are finished, when the last plate has been riveted in place, then that massive steel ship is virtually unsinkable.
>
> Taken by itself, my son's suicide is senseless. Throw it into the sea of Romans 8:28, and it sinks. Still, I believe that when the Eternal Shipbuilder has finally finished, when God has worked out his perfect design, even this senseless tragedy will somehow work to our eternal good.[3]

Prayer helps us see the big picture, especially when the small details do not make sense.

Pray to Resist Temptation to Sin

"Then he returned to his disciples and found them sleeping." Verse 40 begins with these words. They arrest our attention as we consider the momentous decisions being made and the actions being planned that night.[4] Jesus was in one of the toughest spiritual battles of his life. He was planning for victory. The Pharisees had gotten a mob together to arrest Jesus. They were planning for revenge. And the disciples? They were not planning for anything.

Jesus indicated that Peter and the others could not stay awake for even one hour. Before we think too lowly of the disciples, let us remember that all the events of that final week in Jesus' life had been extremely stressful for all. The disciples were fatigued and needed rest. They were exhausted from sorrow. Jesus knew that fatigue pulls people off guard. We are simply not our best and as careful as we should be when we are tired.

Jesus said, "Watch and pray so that you will not fall into temptation. The spirit is willing, but the body is weak." Prayer keeps us on our guard against temptations to sin. Temptation itself is not sin. A temptation is a suggestion or an urge. We cannot always control these, but Jesus warns us to be on our guard against following through with every urge and desire. C.H. Spurgeon, a nineteenth-century British Baptist, used to say, "We cannot help the birds flying over our heads; but we may keep them from building a nest in my hair!"[5]

There are passive sins as well as active sins. Some sins we commit by actually doing something, but others we commit by doing nothing. The sleeping disciples remind us that Christians fall into some sin, not because they do something wrong, but because they do nothing at all. You have probably heard someone pray, "O Lord, please forgive us of the sins of commission and of omission."

"Get real!" a person once told me when I was speaking about prayer. She continued, "Prayer is okay and it makes you feel good. But in the real world it doesn't make any difference. Does prayer really help when we face tough problems?" Her question is important. Yes, prayer really helps us when temptations and trials come. Prayer is not a magic carpet that zips us away from the trouble. It is an internal communication that helps us realize we are not alone in our struggles. Prayer has many beneficial effects. Let us consider one example of the benefits.

Dr. Herbert Benson, a professor at Harvard Medical School, has identified what he calls the "Faith Factor" in physical and emotional healing. The "Faith Factor" is the natural healing process that is made possible by the interaction of two forces. The first is a strong personal belief system that accepts the importance of caring for the body. The second is the practice of prayer and meditation as a part of those beliefs.[6] Benson noticed that people who have firm religious or philosophical convictions and who practice meditative prayer have the most success in healing certain conditions. These include helping to reduce high blood pressure, ease headaches and backaches, and overcome mental depression.

Dr. Kenneth Cooper, the doctor who brought the word *aerobics* into common use, noticed the same thing. Cooper reviewed Benson's work, and the research of others, and came away with these observations:

> As a Christian and a physician, I find such research to be quite encouraging because I do believe that that there is a continuum between natural and supernatural healing. It makes sense to me that deep faith, enhanced by a developed life of prayer and meditation, would have a positive influence on the way our God-given bodies function and heal.[7]

Prayer helps to heal the body and the spirit. It helps us know we are not just some fluke of nature or an orphan in the universe. Prayer is real, and so are its results.

Continue Praying for God's Will

Very little in the spiritual life is easy. Make no mistake about that. Life in the Spirit is often difficult (but, of course, life in general is difficult). The Bible tells us something very important: Jesus himself prayed three different times in his struggle to do God's will. Consider Luke's version of this night. He wrote, "And being in anguish, he prayed more earnestly, and his sweat was like drops of blood falling to the ground" (22:44). That does not sound like a "snap," does it?

What are we to make of this fact? Why would Jesus pray like that? Read the entire story in the New Testament and you will discover that Jesus was a real man. Yes, He was unique—the very Son of God. But he was flesh and blood, too. The early church referred to Jesus as "fully man, fully God." He *struggled* in the garden of Gethsemane about his destiny. The battle going on in his mind was not a sham fight. He wrestled with all the normal human emotions and desires that others have, but he also fought to keep focused on the most important fact, namely, what God willed. Prayer helped Jesus to affirm his mission and continue.

In Matthew 26:42, Jesus prayed a second time. He came to the momentous conclusion of his life and ministry: "My Father, if it is not possible for this cup to be taken away unless I drink it, may your will be done." The key is the phrase, "your will be done." He prayed a third time in a similar manner. After fervent prayer, Jesus was willing to accept whatever was to come. He knew that a cross awaited him.

If Jesus needed to keep praying about doing God's will, what about us? Was he so special and his work so unique that only he had to pray regularly about doing what his Heavenly Father wanted? If Jesus needed it, how much more do we!

What do you really want out of life? Are you striving all alone to achieve your goals? Prayer is not just a tool that allows you to get what you want from life. It is communion with the divine will. As you pray about finding and doing God's will, let the Lord lead you in your life's goals and dreams. Keep praying about this matter.

Jesus prayed not only twice but three times about his decision in the garden of Gethsemane. He prayed about his impending death three times. Some events and decisions in life are too important for quick, shallow thought. They require sustained and repeated prayer. Praying for spiritual strength to do God's will is so important that it needs to be done repeatedly.

Pray to Find Spiritual Strength

If you had been one of Jesus' disciples that night, what would you have done? We might fantasize that we would have stayed awake with Jesus. None of us were there, of course, but we face other trials regularly. Sometimes we are alert and on top, but sometimes we are like old Rip van Winkle, who slept through an entire revolution.

Jesus faced his most trying hour in Gethsemane. His prayers strengthened him to face that time. Our greatest challenges can be met with similar resources.

Praying for spiritual strength to do God's will should include a commitment to do it, no matter what. Jesus was committed to carry out God's will regardless of what it brought. If you pray to discover God's will, be prepared to do it. Otherwise, why bother?

You and I have had heavy blows that nearly sink us. Prayer—honest and open dialogue with the Father—helps us through those times. It certainly has helped me. I was once fired from a church for trying to do the right thing. I had been called to that church with the understanding that I would lead in relocation. I brought in a well-known church consultant who helped with the demographic studies and then assembled a team to guide our transition. The church voted to relocate and we started making plans to begin fund-raising. The next step was to hire a national firm to guide the capital campaign. Just a few days before we signed the contract that would have put us on the road to relocation, I was abruptly fired.

That was the most bitter and painful experience of my life. If I had been dismissed because of a moral lapse, I could have understood that. But a few people decided that the church really should not relocate and they pressured a small group to take drastic action. Not only was I fired from the church, but also one member pressured my civic club to ask me to leave since I was no longer the pastor of the big, influential church. Who ever heard of anyone getting kicked out of a civic club?

I was instantly cut off from my source of spiritual strength—the church—and from my social group—the Rotary Club. A few people tried to erase every trace of my very existence. I told my wife, "It's like they are trying to dig a hole, push me into it, and then cover it over with concrete." With every ounce of strength and determination I could muster, I started a new church from scratch. It is growing slowly and provides the human source of my spiritual strength. These are the strongest, most loving people I have ever known.

I tell this story, not to lash out at the people who injured me, but to make a point. Life is tough and terrible things can happen to us. Prayer—fierce conversations with God—can help us resist the temptation to give in to despair and to abandon our faith. The help of a small group of friends and the living presence of God were the only things that got my wife and me through this terrible ordeal. It really does matter.

It's Your Turn Now

What is the one most challenging issue facing you right now? Based on this study of Jesus' example of prayer, design a prayer strategy to deal with this challenge.

- What are some of your biggest challenges in life right now?
- What is God's will for your challenges listed above? How can you keep on praying until you find God's will and his strength to assist you in this dilemma?
- Think of some of the struggles and temptations you have faced over the past two weeks. Did prayer help you in any of them?
- If you did not pray during those times, make up your mind now to ask for God's help this week as you face whatever comes your way.

Questions for Further Reflection

1. Think of the cartoon mentioned at the beginning of this chapter. Can you identify with it?
2. Why do you think Jesus prayed so earnestly over his decision in the garden of Gethsemane?
3. In what ways can prayer help you during times of temptation?
4. Reflect on the research of Dr. Herbert Benson and Dr. Kenneth Cooper regarding the relation of faith, prayer, and health. Are there any changes you might need to make in your life to maximize the benefits of faith and prayer?
5. What does the "miracle of the shipyard" say to you and your experiences? How does God put things together to make them "float"?

8

Prayer and God's Will for Your Life

Be very careful, then, how you live—not as unwise but as wise, making the most of every opportunity, because the days are evil. Therefore do not be foolish, but understand what the Lord's will is. Do not get drunk on wine, which leads to debauchery. Instead, be filled with the Spirit. Speak to one another with psalms, hymns and spiritual songs. Sing and make music in your heart to the Lord, always giving thanks to God the Father for everything, in the name of our Lord Jesus Christ. Submit to one another out of reverence for Christ.

EPHESIANS 5:15–21

We have been looking at the biblical concept of prayer throughout this book. We began by looking at some of the common misunderstandings about prayer. Then we considered the invitation that comes to each of us to become people of prayer. Next, we looked at one way of praying and then we explored the importance of our attitude to our prayer life. We also looked at the fact that others need our prayers as much as we do. Then we examined the life of Jeremiah to see the open, almost shocking, honesty needed for prayer.

Now we are going to pull together much of what we examined earlier and ask this simple question: *Where does prayer fit in with*

God's will for my life? Let us do this by briefly exploring the general nature of God's will.

God's General Will

There is much confusion about the concept of God's will. Some people think of God's will as being a target with a bull's-eye. The key, they think, is to fire at the target and hit the center every time. Any shot outside the bull's-eye is thus a shot outside of God's perfect will. But is that really an accurate image of God's will? I do not believe it is.

To begin with, we need to reexamine some of the phrases that are often used in connection with God's will, phrases such as "God showed me," "discern the Lord's mind," "the very center of his will," and so on. Theologian Gary Friesen makes a strong statement about these and other like phrases. He writes, "Such terminology reflects the conviction that the key to making the 'right' decision is discernment of God's ideal plan. What is so striking, as one searches the pages of the New Testament, is the *glaring absence* of such expressions."[1]

Friesen points out that the New Testament does not approach the will of God with the metaphor of an archer hitting a bull's-eye. Instead, it pictures Christians who use their minds to perceive what God has revealed for all people. Friesen's argument flows as follows:

> In the progress of His revelation, God moved from a highly structured system of regulations governing a wide range of specific behaviors to a system where behavior is to be determined by principles and governed by personal relationship. There was a progress from law to Christ; from the bondage of close, restrictive supervision appropriate to immature and willful children to the freedom of responsible adulthood."[2]

The apostle Paul wrote about our movement from the restrictive bondage of childhood to the open freedom of Christ. Read his comments in Galatians 4:1–11. This kind of mature freedom is not possible for everyone, of course. I wrote these words at a church camp in Ridgecrest, N.C. Outside my window several young adults were busy sweeping the walks and picking up trash. All of them were mentally challenged. A supervisor stayed with them all the time to offer specific guidance. The young people needed it. But if those employees had been mature and capable of handling themselves, having a supervisor stand over them and tell them everything to do would have been irritating and degrading. Mature people think for themselves and make their own decisions from many options.

God nurtures us toward maturity. In that maturity, coupled with the wisdom he gives us, we are responsible for making wise decisions from all the possibilities that come our way.

I think Friesen is onto something here. He articulated what others have noticed, too. God intends his children to grow up and use their wisdom to discover what God wants them to do. Many people approach the idea of God's will as if they think that all people remain infants who need to be taken by the hand and walked all the way through life. But the Scriptures call us to grow up in our faith and to use our God-given wisdom to live a wholesome, well-rounded life in relationship to God and to other people.

But does God have a minutely detailed plan for every person? Friesen says, "If God's plan is thought of as a blueprint or 'dot' in the 'center of God's will' that must be discovered by the decision maker, the answer is no. On the other hand, we affirm that God does have a plan for our lives—a plan that is described in the Bible in terms that we can fully understand and apply."[3] I agree. On the whole, the Bible does not give us a prescription for finding the "center of God's will." What it does is to call us into relationship with God through Christ, and then challenges us to live according to what he has *already* revealed.

Think about it this way. The late English theologian John Oman said that God does not do his work like an archer firing his arrows straight into a target. Instead, God works the way rain falls onto the mountains and then finds its way down into streams and through rivers into the oceans. The water ultimately reaches the ocean, but the trip could have been made through many routes. To apply that analogy to our lives, when we give ourselves to God through faith and prayer, God's will is ultimately achieved. However, in the meantime he allows human beings to participate in its accomplishment.[4]

The traditional approach to thinking about God's will is almost a "needle-in-a-haystack" approach. The sheer number of factors that could be involved is mind-boggling. Take the idea of finding a mate, for example. Some people say that God has one person already prepared for everyone—a "Mr. Right" or a "Miss Right." But the logistics of finding that one person out of so many possibilities is overwhelming. If a person does not find that one perfect mate, does that mean he or she has sinned and is out of God's will by marrying someone else? I do not think so. Instead of only one person being a potential mate, there may be many. To find God's will in the matter is to take seriously what the revealed will of God—the Bible—teaches us about Christian marriage. For example, we are not to be yoked with an unbeliever (2 Cor. 6:14); we are to have mutual respect for our mate (Eph. 5:21–33), and so on. More than one person will fit these criteria. Our job is to make mature, thoughtful decisions about the matter. Do I love and respect this person? Does he or she have the personal qualities that I admire and make me want to spend my life with that person? Prayer in these types of matters helps to clarify our thoughts and to center us on what is really important.

Choosing a Life Path That Is Pleasing to God

Allow me to share a personal story about this. My discovery of the wonder and mystery of losing myself in the life of someone else came, like many of life's good things, unexpectedly. I took a semester away from college during my second year and worked in a Christian coffee house across the street from the university. I had made a commitment to the Lord and had felt a "call" to ministry. At the time I had no idea what that might mean, so I took some time to explore options.

One of the options was to attend a Christian college. I applied for admission to Louisiana College, a Baptist school in the center of Louisiana, and was accepted. I arrived on campus in the fall of 1971 not knowing a soul, but having more enthusiasm than I had ever known before. Several people told me that the course of study would be harder than that of the large university, and they were right. The classes were smaller, the professors got to know their students, and they expected a lot of work. It was that first year there that I made many discoveries about truth, life, and myself. One of these latter discoveries was that I had a mind and could use it. After all, Jesus had said that we were to love God with our entire mind.

That first year at Louisiana College came to a close and I faced its end with much regret. Never before had a place and a group of people become so much a part of me. But I had no money for summer school so I had to go to work.

My brother and his wife invited me to stay with them. He was working for a large chemical plant in Freeport, Texas, and felt sure I could get on with them. I packed a few clothes and caught a ride to their home in the little community of Oyster Creek. The day I arrived, the plant was closed by a strike!

I began scrounging around for a job—any job. School in the fall would be expensive, and there was no time to fool around. The only thing I found was a job selling vacuum cleaners door to door. What a predicament for a budding young theologian! I went out every day with people I did not especially like, tried to sell a product that I thought was overpriced, lived in a cramped trailer with my brother and his wife, and felt more alone than I had ever felt in my life. I attended a church in Freeport several times, and each time I filled out the little card and checked the box, "I would like the pastor to visit me." I wanted to talk to someone, but no one from the church ever called or came by. Besides all that, I was not making much money.

A new fellow showed up at the office one day. We young salesmen were told in almost reverent tones about the selling skill of this man, so I looked forward to meeting him. I was not impressed. He and I just did not "click" at first, so I simply avoided him when I could. After all, I thought my time there was very temporary, so why take time to try to befriend someone I did not immediately like? A few months would pass and I would return to school and never see this fellow again. However, "The best laid plans of mice and men…"

One day after work this new man invited me to our employer's house, where he and his family were staying temporarily. I showed up at the appointed time and rang the doorbell and a girl answered. I am always suspicious of people who claim, "love at first sight" but I surely was impressed with her. It was not love, but it sure was interest. I learned that this girl was the daughter of the super salesman. She was my age, also a college student, and also uprooted for the summer by their move from Oklahoma to Texas. Had her father just "happened" to invite me over because he liked me, or could it be...? I was beginning to suspect something.

As it turned out I should have, but I was not being set up for pain. This girl, whose name was Carla, became my friend, my confidant, someone who shared many of my interests and outlooks. We began spending every spare minute together and, although both of us resisted it, felt that we were being drawn closer and closer together. After all, we had come together almost by accident, were students at schools hundreds of miles apart, and hardly had the money for a hamburger between us. How could anything possibly come of that?

My summer of isolation in Texas drew to a close, and I had mixed feelings about it. I was glad to be getting away from a job I so thoroughly disliked, and looked forward to going back into an academic setting. But this girl...

Two people coming to love each other is a mysterious event. Logic has its place in the event, but loving is not primarily logical. My keeping an interest in this girl whose father had once been my boss, and who lived hundreds of miles away, was anything but logical.

We went our separate ways that fall, but ran up large phone and postage bills. Finally, toward the end of that semester we both knew it was time to make a serious decision—end the relationship or make a commitment to each other regarding our future. With a little fear, and a whole lot of youthful zeal, we decided that Carla would transfer from her university to join me at my college. This decision changed us for the rest of our lives. We married our last semester at Louisiana College, and lived on love. We had to because we did not have any money. Carla sorted letters at the post office part time and I was the stockman for the auto parts department at Sears. Between us, we made enough to pay our $35 per week rent on two rooms, to eat a frozen dinner each evening (that we bought three for a dollar), and to pay for books and supplies at school. Carla also worked in the cafeteria and I tutored in the religion department to make a few extra dollars. Our loans and scholarships paid tuition. Most of all, we had each other. What else mattered? If that sounds like the making of a cheap novel, so be it. It was (and still is) true for us and we knew that, whatever came, our commitment to each other would pull us through, and it has.

Carla and I have been married over thirty years now. We are the parents of twin sons, Ryan and Christopher—the former in medical school at the University of Miami and the latter working on a doctorate at Christ Church, Oxford University, England. How can I refer to any of that as planned, logical, or ordinary? Yet, in its own way, this is exactly what it is. Our story is unique in its details, but many, many people have had similar experiences of coming to love. People who did not even like each other at first later end up "hitched." I can think of a couple who are friends of ours, and the man was the woman's high school teacher. Later they married and today have one of the strongest families I know. Another couple began their relationship with the man being the woman's supervisor in a hospital lab.

The point of this is that Carla and I had a choice in the matter. We do feel there was some providence involved, but we had to take the risk and make the choices about our lives. No one, not even God, will make your decisions for you. God certainly did not force us to marry, and we could have married others instead. The choice was ours to make.

I told the story at the beginning of chapter 4 of the young man who wanted me to pray that God would immediately send him a wife. That way of going about the business of getting a wife is clearly immature and foolish. God expects us to grow up in our faith, to make wise, mature decisions about all areas of life. J.I. Packer defines wisdom this way: "Wisdom is the power to see, and the inclination to choose, the best and the highest goal, together with the surest means of attaining it."[5] Gaining this wisdom takes humility, work, and patience. The characteristics of biblical wisdom include reverence, humility, teachableness, diligence, uprightness, and faith. Gary Friesen writes about this wisdom as follows:

> The Christian *attitude* is to reflect, first of all, his awareness that no man, himself included, is naturally wise in himself (Proverbs 3:7); and therefore, if he is to gain wisdom, it

must come from some other source. Equally, his attitude must mirror his conviction that the ultimate source of wisdom is God alone. Those who refuse to acknowledge these basic realities are self-deceived fools (Romans 1:21–22). But the posture of the one who would find wisdom is that of bowing.[6]

Wisdom is necessary to make good decisions in life. Humility and asking for it in prayer are necessary to gain wisdom. Prayer is necessary to gain humility and wisdom. Thus prayer is essential to making decisions that affect our lives. Let us now think about how all of this relates specifically to finding God's will.

God's Specific Will

T. B. Maston, through his classroom and his writings, taught an entire generation of pastors. He zeroed in on an important aspect of God's will. He wrote:

It will help a great deal as we seek to know the will of God if prayer becomes the practice of our lives. This means, among other things, that we shall have some regular prayer habits that have become fixed patterns in our lives. It should be just as unthinkable to start the day for the Lord without some time for communion with him as it would be to begin the work of the day without our regular morning routine or preparation for the day.[7]

Finding the will of God is not nearly as difficult as some people claim. God has a general will for everyone. Paul wrote to the Ephesian Christians, "Therefore do not be foolish, but understand what the Lord's will is" (5:17). Earlier he had said to them, "For I have not hesitated to proclaim to you the whole will of God" (Acts 20:27). How did Paul know "the whole will of God" for the Ephesians? He knew because God's will for them is the same as for everyone else. For example, "The Lord is not slow in keeping his promise, as some understand slowness. He is patient with you, not wanting anyone to perish, but everyone to come to repentance" (2 Pet. 3:9). To young Timothy, Paul wrote, "This is good, and pleases God our Savior, who wants all men to be saved and to come to a knowledge of the truth"

(1 Tim. 2:3–4). That, on the whole, is what God wants. One theologian put it this way: "God's purpose is to create a worldwide family of persons who freely accept God as their God and who receive his love into their lives, and who respond to him by loving him with all their hearts and loving their neighbors as themselves."[8]

God thus wants people to be saved. Salvation comes about when people give themselves completely to God and allow him to transform them in the likeness of Christ. We learn about that desire from the Bible and from the lives of other Christians. We should be very careful about other purely subjective means of knowing something about God and his will. One scholar wrote, "Christians…do not behold a pillar of fire for assurance of God's presence. Nor do they consult the Urim and Thummim for His direction. Instead, they rely on the Word of God for both."[9]

So God desires salvation for all people. We participate in that salvation when we accept it as God's gift, and as we pray that others might become open to it also. As we "grow up" in our faith and prayer life, we become less self-oriented and more God-oriented. Fisher Humphreys said of this orientation toward God:

> Because he loves us, he will hear when we speak to him on any topic we care about. But precisely because he loves us so much, he wants us to become concerned about his "adult" purpose. Ideally, our prayer should more and more be about achieving his purpose. We ought to be talking to him about the community, about its growth in faith and love, about the freedom of mankind, about the proclamation of the good news about Jesus.[10]

We pray for God's will, which is "not an attempt to second guess God, asking for what God was going to do anyway. It is rather talking to God about achieving his purpose, and asking him to do those things which we believe will carry forward his purpose."[11]

T. B. Maston echoes this idea. He wrote:

> As we mature in prayer, we shall discover that we shall be more alert to and less uncertain about the will of

God for our lives. We shall pray less for ourselves and more that God's will might be done in the world. Our conception of his will will become more inclusive. The maturing Christian also prays less that he may know the will of God and more that he may be used by the Lord to do his will in the world. In other words, he becomes less self-centered and more God-centered.[12]

What this means is that we will not always get our way. Prayer will not be a tool for prying out of God what he is unwilling to give. What he is willing to give is fullness in our spiritual lives (see Jn. 10:10), and a sense of wholeness despite our circumstances. One man looked at his circumstances and realized he was more that the sum of such circumstances. That man was John Quincy Adams. On the occasion of his eightieth birthday, he said:

> John Quincy Adams is well. The house in which he lives at present is dilapidated. It is tottering upon its foundation. Time and the seasons have nearly destroyed it. Its roof is pretty well worn out. Its walls are much shattered and it trembles with every wind. I think John Quincy Adams will have to move out of it soon. But he himself is well, quite well.[13]

That captures the spirit of the Christians who live close to God through prayer and through wanting what God wants. That keeps life from shrinking in on itself until the soul resembles a prune. One lady began investing in the stock market in 1944 and kept doing so until her death at age 101 in 1995. She built a portfolio worth $22 million! But she lived a loveless, shallow life. Someone who knew her said, "a big day for her was walking down to Merrill Lynch...to visit her stock certificates."[14] She seems to have lived a wasted life because close relationships to others and love for God were lacking.

Making Specific Decisions

How do we make specific decisions as we seek God's will? Remember that we are not Moses who can go up on the mountain and return with the answer written in stone. We live by faith. As we pray and seek God's will in specific matters, keep in mind that "God has not promised to whisper 'perfect plans' or omniscience into the mind of any believer who asks."[15] In general, the narrow road may be wider than you think (Mt. 7:14). *Many possibilities exist before us.* Many choices are equally valid. As mature Christians we are to weigh the choices, apply basic principles for decision-making, and make a mature choice. I realize this statement goes against what many people say they believe. They think that there is one, and only one, right choice in any matter, ranging from the clothes they wear today to the career they have to the person they marry. I do not believe that, on the whole, the Bible, and in particular the New Testament, supports such a concept. Strong leading by God *does* seem to occur in some circumstances, but those events seem to be the exception rather than the rule.

Gary Friesen has developed a set a principles for decision making that I find helpful. He calls this the way of wisdom. Consider these as you prayerfully seek God's will for your life and as you make decisions.[16]

1. In areas specifically addressed by the Bible, the revealed commands and principles of God are to be obeyed. This is his moral will. For example, the Bible reveals God's will about telling the truth (Ex. 20:16). We never need to pray and ask, "Lord, should I tell the truth?" That matter is already settled. Again, the Bible reveals God's will about taking care of family (1 Tim. 5:8). The specific details of how we do that are left up to us, but the command to care for our family is not.

Some matters, then, are clearly spelled out. If we are told by the Scripture to do them, then do them. If we are told not to do them, avoid them.

2. In those areas for which the Bible gives no command or principle (as in nonmoral decisions), the believer is free and responsible to choose his own course of action. Any decision made within the moral will of God is acceptable to God. For example, I wrote these words on my personal laptop computer that I take with me when I travel. The Bible gives no guidance on this type of technology. Would writing this book in pencil be more

spiritual or godly than using a computer? Not necessarily. It is simply not an issue dealt with in Scripture. I believe that God expects me to examine all the factors and then make a wise decision about it on my own. Since I do a great deal of writing, having a computer is much more efficient and helpful than trying to write in longhand. I actually wrote several major projects that way and can testify to the efficiency of the computer.

3. In nonmoral decisions, the objective of the Christian is to make wise decisions on the basis of spiritual expediency. After weighing all the factors involved, the right decision is one that will be the most Christ-honoring. Sometimes one choice is clearly called for, but sometimes more than one choice will fit this criterion.

For example, a young person might be considering the choices among several colleges. After examining them carefully, this student discovers they are all about the same and that any of them would offer a good education in a spiritually healthy environment. How does he or she choose? Does she or he ask God to send a sign from heaven? God wants children who are willing to go wherever God leads. However, sometimes God lets us make the choices ourselves. In the case of such students, they need to ask themselves where they really want to go, and then go there.

4. In all decisions, the believer should humbly submit, in advance, to the outworking of God's sovereign will as it touches each decision. When Carla and I decided to marry, we trusted God with the results of our decision. In the example above, the student needs to make a choice about a college and then trust the consequences of that decision to God's sovereign purpose.

Keep in mind that even seemingly negative consequences can be the results of God's sovereignty. Not everything associated with God is soft. For example, Joe Aldrich was President of Multnomah Bible College and Seminary when he was diagnosed with Parkinson's disease. Is that disease a result of sin or negligence? Could prayer remove it?

Consider Aldrich's own view:

> In my case I believe that Parkinson's is a custom-made instrument of grace to help me toward servanthood. Through eyes of faith I see it as a wake-up call from a loving heavenly Father. Does prayer really make a difference? Yes! I perceive that Parkinson's is an instrument that God is using to answer some of my prayers. It is deepening my confidence in God—that's an answer to prayer. It is enriching my relationship with Ruthe—that's an answer to prayer. It is broadening my understanding and my appreciation of those who are hurting—and that's an answer to prayer. It is teaching me dependence—and that's an answer to prayer. It is teaching me to pray—and that's an answer to prayer.[17]

We should be careful not to assume that if we search for God's will, we will find only happiness. God is in the process of helping people conform to the likeness of his Son. That likeness includes strengthening through trials. (See 2 Cor. 4:1–17.) Aldrich observed, "Most of us, it seems, don't really want God to love us—we want him to be kind to us, to mature us without pain, to teach us servanthood without serving, to develop patience without trials."[18]

Our prayers help cause things to happen and matters to take different courses. When we pray, we work in correspondence with God's sovereignty to affect our lives. This does not happen easily. Prayer is work.

Learn to take your chances with God. Pray. Prayer does not change God's ultimate will, but it allows you to lay hold on his willingness. It will not keep you from making mistakes and from taking your share of hard knocks, but prayer will bring you close to the heavenly Father who loves you more than words can describe. Ecclesiastes 9:10 says, "Whatever your hand finds to do, do it with all your might…" That includes living and praying and making your choices in life, and then accepting the consequences.

God wants the best for you. Why choose anything less?

It's Your Turn Now

- Give some thought about what you consider your life's mission.
- Do you think of that mission as God-directed?
- Write out a life-plan for the next twelve months.
- List some of the choices you face and include all of the options that seem to be viable.
- Talk to someone you consider to be spiritually mature about decisions you need to make.
- Reread all of the Scripture passages cited in this chapter.
- Develop a regular habit of praying about all of the major decisions in your life.

Questions for Further Reflection

1. Which is more helpful as you think about finding God's will: the imagery of a target with a bull's-eye, or the imagery of rain falling on the mountain and finding its way to the ocean?
2. How do you react to the concept of making "adult" decisions? Is that a helpful suggestion?
3. Have you ever spent much time searching for God's will only to feel like you were searching for a "needle in a haystack"?
4. What do you think is God's general will for your life?
5. This statement is made above: "The narrow road may be wider than you think." What do you think that means?
6. Gary Friesen gives four principles for decision making. Do you agree with what he said, or do you think something is lacking?
7. Consider the things Joe Aldrich said he learned from his illness. Has anything in your life taught you similar things?
8. Do you think God really loves you and wants the best for you?

Conclusion

Although I call this section a "conclusion," that can be misleading. A conclusion could be seen as meaning the same thing as "the end," and I emphatically do not intend that. Quite the opposite. I intend this section to wrap up some of our thinking throughout the book, but then to be the doorway into the active work of praying.

Theory is fine and necessary for any activity or process. I would not want to fly on a plane built by a designer who did not know the theories of wind resistance, metal stress tolerance, and jet propulsion. But halting at theory is no good. If that were the case in the aircraft industry, we would all still be walking. Somewhere along the way we move from theory and background knowledge to actually doing what we have been training for all along.

We have been thinking about prayer throughout this book. While we have considered the biblical background of prayer and its theology, we must not stop there. We need to move to the level of incorporating what we have learned into an on-going experience. I introduced you to the concept of prayer as a "fierce conversation," one that moves beyond the pleasantries of surface chatter to the depths of intense dialogue with the heavenly Father.

Everything is fair game in prayer...*everything.* Do you have a hurt so deep that the mere thought of it forms a lump in your throat and stings your eyes with tears? That is a subject for prayer as you pour your hurt, anger, disappointment, and fear out to the One who loves hearing from you more than you can imagine. Do you revel in a joy so intimate that it bubbles to the surface at the most unexpected times? That is a subject for prayer as you laugh and wrap yourself in a relationship with the Creator who revels in your joy. Prayer is reasonable, but, more than that, it is also life at the depths. It is the breadth of human experience. It is the focal point for God's interaction with mankind in general and you in particular.

I was on a trip to Australia once when a strange thing happened. Our flight was somewhere over the Pacific Ocean at about 3:00 a.m. Most of the passengers were asleep when a recorded announcement began sounding throughout the plane. It said, "We have experienced an emergency. You must use oxygen now. We are descending to a safe altitude but you must use oxygen now." You can imagine how abruptly everyone woke up. We began looking for the oxygen masks but none came from the overhead compartments. I thought that whatever problem caused the loss of oxygen was now being compounded by the fact that the oxygen masks would not drop into place. The crew hurried into the cabin and had everyone's undivided attention! After a few minutes the captain came on the intercom and apologized for the announcement. He said there was no oxygen emergency and no one could find out why the warning had played at all. Eventually most of us went back to sleep, but I have never forgotten those moments between hearing the warning and the realization that I could not find the oxygen mask, and then finally getting the all-clear from the pilot.

Some people seem to live their entire lives in the crisis mode between the warning and the all-clear. That is a genuine shame because it is unnecessary. Sure, we will have many crises and setbacks, but the simple fact is this: *We are not alone in our difficulties.* Psalm 34:18 puts it this way. "The LORD is close to the brokenhearted / and saves those who are crushed in spirit." How close is God? As close as prayer.

Throughout this book I have invited you to pray. You do not need to be a "professional" or anything of the like. Just start. With both humility and gratitude reach out to God in the way you would reach out to a best friend or trusted loved one. Pray about everything—all of your needs and those of your family and friends; your work and the decisions you make; others around you who need your prayers, even if you do not know them personally; and yes, even for those you might consider enemies. Be honest and keep it real. You are not trying to impress God with your eloquence.

As we close, I would like to pray for you. Please read the following as my prayer for you.

Dear Lord,

Thank you for the invitation to dialogue with you in the deepest recesses of our hearts. We're grateful for the privilege of your willingness to hear any and every concern we bring to you.

Father, you know us better than we know ourselves, and you love us greater than any other human being we know. You know the needs of the readers of this book. You know what they desire. You know their confusion and fear. You are aware of their pleasures, passions, and joy.

Help all of us learn to pray. Draw us into a deeper communion with you. Take all that we have to offer and whisper in our spirits, "Well done, good and faithful servant."

Now Father, bless the writer and the reader, both of whom need your touch. Let the disciplines of reaching out to you become our life-long habit. Teach us to pray.

In Jesus' name, Amen.

Don M. Aycock

(Please feel free to contact Don through his Web site: www.donaycock.net.)

Notes

Introduction

[1]Cited in Herbert Benson, M.D., with Marg Stark, *Timeless Healing: The Power and Biology of Belief* (New York: Scribner, 1996), 173.

[2]Blaise Pascal, *Pensées,* trans. A. J. Krailsheimer (London: Penguin Classics, 1966), 127.

[3]Information obtained from http://www.quotationspage.com/quotes/Anne-Sophie Swetchine, on November 29, 2005.

Chapter 1: You Are Invited to Pray

[1]Alex Haley, quoted in Walter Anderson, *The Greatest Risk of All* (Boston: Houghton Mifflin Co., 1988), 240.

[2]David Whyte, quoted in Susan Scott, *Fierce Conversations: Achieving Success at Work & in Life, One Conversation at a Time* (New York: Berkley Books, 2002), 6.

[3]Scott, *Fierce Conversations,* 6.

[4]Ibid., 7.

[5]Harry Emerson Fosdick, *The Meaning of Prayer,* quoted in Bob Benson Sr. and Michael W. Benson, *Disciplines for the Inner Life,* rev. ed. (Nashville: Thomas Nelson Publishers, 1989), 40.

[6]Donald G. Bloesch, *The Struggle of Prayer* (San Francisco: Harper & Row, 1980), 158.

[7]Leon Morris, *The Gospel According to St. Luke,* Tyndale New Testament Commentaries (Grand Rapids: Eerdmans, 1974), 195.

[8]Theodore Roosevelt, quoted in Anderson, *The Greatest Risk of All,* 3.

[9]From a newspaper ad published in Bogalusa, La., 1980.

[10]Wilfred Wilkinson, *Good News in Luke* (Glasgow: William Collins Sons, 1974), 72.

[11]Information obtained from http://www.sermonillustrations.com/a-z/u/unexpected.htm on November 29, 2005.

[12]G. B. Caird, *Saint Luke,* The Pelican New Testament Commentaries (Baltimore: Penguin Books, 1963), 152.

[13]Herbert Bensen, M.D., with Marg Stark, *Timeless Healing: The Power and Biology of Belief* (New York: Scribner, 1996), 196.

[14]Ibid., 197.

[15]Ibid., 300.

[16]George A. Buttrick, *Prayer* (New York: Abingdon-Cokesbury Press, 1943), 85–86.

Chapter 2: A Stubborn Misunderstanding of Prayer

[1]George Appleton, *Journey for a Soul* (Glasgow: William Collins Sons & Co.), 199–200.

[2]Richard B. Gardner, *Matthew,* Believers Church Bible Commentary (Scottsdale: Herald Press, 1991), 318.

[3]For more on this see Don M. Aycock, *Eight Days That Changed the World* (Grand Rapids: Kregel Publications, 1997), chapter 2.

[4]John Marks Templeton, *The Templeton Plan: 21 Steps to Success and Happiness, as described by John Marks Templeton to James Ellison* (San Francisco: Harper & Row, 1987), ix.

[5]Ross Phares, *Bible in Pocket, Gun in Hand: The Story of Frontier Religion* (Lincoln: University of Nebraska Press, 1971 [1964]), 6.

⁶Information obtained from http://steelguitarforum.com/Forum14/HTML/ 002491.html on November 29, 2005.
⁷Frederick Douglass, "Narrative of the Life of Frederick Douglass," in *The Classic Slave Narratives,* ed. and introd. by Henry Louis Gates, Jr. (New York: Penguin Books USA, 1987), 286.
⁸C. S. Lewis, quoted in "Does Prayer Really Change Things?" in *Faith* (February/ March 1989): 8.
⁹"Magic," in *The American Heritage Dictionary of the English Language,* ed. William Morris (Boston: Houghton Mifflin Co., 1969).
¹⁰Dick Rice, quoted by Kenneth L. Woodward in "Why America Prays," *Reader's Digest* (April 1992): 200.
¹¹C. S. Lewis, quoted in Rueben P. Job and Norman Shawchuck, *A Guide to Prayer* (Nashville: The Upper Room, 1983), 85.

Chapter 3: Pray Like This

¹Patty Roberts, *Ashes To Gold* (Waco, Tex.: Word Books, 1983), 78.
²Fisher Humphreys, "Christian Prayer," *The Student* (August 1985): 27.
³Richard J. Foster, *Prayer: Finding the Heart's True Home* (San Francisco: HarperSanFrancisco, 1992), 8–9.
⁴Fisher Humphreys, *The Heart of Prayer* (New Orleans: Insight Press, 1980), 89.
⁵From "Paraphrase of Sorts" in *Pulpit Digest* (September-October 1979): 56.
⁶C. S. Lewis, "Does Prayer Really Change Things?" *Faith* (February/March 1989): 9.
⁷Quoted in ibid.,9.
⁸Robert H. Mounce, *Matthew: A Good News Commentary* (San Francisco: Harper & Row, 1985), 54.
⁹Booker T. Washington, *Up from Slavery* (1901; reprint, West Berlin, N.J.: Townsend Press, 2004).
¹⁰Winston Churchill, quoted in Kenneth H. Cooper, *It's Better To Believe* (Nashville: Thomas Nelson, 1995), 31.

Chapter 4: Your Attitude Is Important

¹Samuel Johnson, quoted in Og Mandino, *Secrets For Success and Happiness* (New York: Fawcett Columbine, 1995), 240.
²Chris Browne, "Hagar The Horrible," King Features Syndicate, December 21, 1994.
³Robert Coles, "The Inexplicable Prayers of Ruby Bridges," *Christianity Today* (August 9, 1985): 19.
⁴Ibid., 20.
⁵John Bunyan, quoted in Don Aycock, *How to Have a Conversation with God: Prayer That Draws Us Closer to the Father* (Grand Rapids: Kregel Publications, 2004), 43.
⁶Fisher Humphreys, *The Heart of Prayer* (New Orleans: Insight Press, 1980), 55–56.
⁷Ibid., 57–58.
⁸Alister McGrath, *Mystery of the Cross* (Grand Rapids: Academie Books, 1988), cited in Mark K. Yarbrough, "When God Doesn't Heal," *Christianity Today* (September 2004): 80.

Chapter 5: Others Need Your Prayers

¹Lewis Grizzard, "A Miracle of Recovery Called Prayer," May 13, 1993, from his syndicated newspaper column.
²Ibid.

[3]Blaise Pascal, quoted in Og Mandino, *Secrets for Success and Happiness* (New York: Fawcett Columbine, 1995), 200.

[4]Henry David Thoreau, quoted in Mandino, *Secrets for Success,* unnumbered preface page.

[5]Charles H. Rabon, "Be Still and Know—an Experiment in Prayer," *Quarterly Review* (January-March, 1988): 35.

[6]Frank Wright, "The Power of Personal Holiness" *NRB* (November/December 2004): 4.

[7]Saint Patrick, as quoted by John W. Cowart, in "The Real Saint Patrick," *Catholic Digest* (March 1984): 19.

[8]Ibid.

[9]This letter is from Bruce Larsen, *Dare To Live Now* (Grand Rapids: Zondervan, 1965), 83.

Chapter 6: Honesty in Prayer

[1]James Leo Green, "Jeremiah," *The Broadman Bible Commentary,* vol. 6 (Nashville: Broadman Press, 1971), 81.

[2]Ibid., 110.

[3]C. S. Lewis, "Does Prayer Really Change Things?" in *Faith* (February-March, 1989): 8.

[4]Elizabeth Achtemeier, *Jeremiah,* Knox Preaching Guides (Atlanta: John Knox Press, 1987), 64.

Chapter 7: God Will Strengthen You through Prayer

[1]Curtis C. Mitchell, "Why Keep Bothering God?" *Christianity Today* (December 13, 1985): 34.

[2]P. T. Forsyth, quoted in Mitchell, "Why Keep Bothering God?" 34.

[3]Quoted in Richard Exley, "Decent Exposure," *Leadership* (Fall 1992): 118.

[4]For more on this night in Jesus' life, see Don Aycock, *Eight Days That Changed The World* (Grand Rapids: Kregel Publications, 1997). This book examines the last week of Jesus' life, from Palm Sunday to Easter Sunday.

[5]C.H. Spurgeon, quoted in Barbara Ehrenreich, "Welcome to Cancerland," *Harper's Magazine* (November 2001): 48.

[6]These findings are from Dr. Herbert Benson, *The Relaxation Response* (New York: Morrow, 1975), and are well summarized by Dr. Kenneth Cooper in *It's Better To Believe* (Nashville: Thomas Nelson, Inc., 1995), 28. Also see another of Benson's books (with Marg Stark), *Timeless Healing: The Power of Biology and Belief* (New York: Scribner, 1996).

[7]Cooper, *It's Better To Believe,* 28.

Chapter 8: Prayer and God's Will for Your Life

[1]Gary Friesen, with J. Robin Maxson, *Decision Making and the Will of God: A Biblical Alternative to the Traditional Approach* (Portland: Multnomah Press, 1980), 182. Italics author's.

[2]Ibid., 86.

[3]Ibid., 113.

[4]For further discussion on this, see Fisher Humphreys, *The Heart of Prayer* (New Orleans: Insight Press, 1980), 54–55.

[5]J.I. Packer , quoted in Friesen, *Decision Making,* 188.

[6]Friesen, *Decision Making,* 193.

[7]T. B. Maston, *God's Will and Your Life* (Nashville: Broadman Press, 1964), 73.

[8]Fisher Humphreys, *Heart of Prayer,* 89.

[9]Friesen, *Decision Making,* 245.

[10]Humphreys, *Heart of Prayer,* 92.

[11]Ibid., 93.

[12]Maston, *God's Will,* 73–74.

[13]John Quincy Adams, quoted in John F. MacArthur, *The Glory of Heaven: The Truth about Heaven, Angels and Eternal Life* (Wheaton: Crossway Books, 1996), 52.

[14]See the cover story in *Money* magazine, January 1996.

[15]Friesen, *Decision Making,* 261.

[16]Ibid., 257.

[17]Joe C. Aldrich, "When Bad News Comes," *Decision* (April 1996): 32–33.

[18]Ibid.